Unleashing
the Power of
Unconditional
Respect

What Top Professionals in the Field are Saying about this Book

" ... a must-read for anyone serious about exploring leadership in policing and creating positive paradigm shifts within police organizations.... This content can save an officer's career, improve overall effectiveness and efficiency within a department, and build community trust and relations—even in minority communities, where typically, trust is lowest and relations are most strained. ... very progressive in its discussion of typically sensitive topics.... "

—**Major Randy Hopkins**
Executive Officer, Administration Bureau
Kansas City, Missouri, Police Department

"This important and even unsettling book is a clarion call to rethink how the police serve the public."

—**Dr. Gary Armstrong**
Professor of Political Science
William Jewell College
Liberty, Missouri

"Colwell and Huth have struck a chord of innovation and crispness which will assuredly provide a working framework for police authorities as they engage the challenges of policing dynamic communities of the twenty-first century."

—**Michael Birzer**
Director and Associate Professor
School of Community Affairs
Wichita State University

"The concepts of integrity, courage, and unconditional respect for all are critical elements in the development of law enforcement professionals, yet they reflect a gap in many of today's law enforcement training programs. This book is a positive step towards filling that gap."

—**Brian Willis, President, Winning Mind Training**

"This book inspired me; all Americans should read it."

—**Debra Sheffer, Ph.D.**
Associate Professor, History
Chair, University Assessment Committee
Park University

"Colwell and Huth seek nothing less than to effect a transformation of how we educate and train police officers. Their argument is well grounded, well supported, and compelling. This will be a classic in leadership education for first responders and any who seek to serve and protect."

—**Colonel Gregory Fontenot, U.S. Army (Retired)**
Former Director of the School of Advanced Military Studies
Director of the University of Foreign Military Studies
Coauthor of On Point: The US Army in Operation Iraqi Freedom

"Colwell and Huth present us with an amalgam of theory, best practices, and sound advice that if followed, will lead us down the path of transformation. We would do well to follow the map that they have provided for us."

—**Chief Gregory P. Mills**
Director of Public Safety
Riverside, Missouri

"I have undergone a training regimen this year that includes the precepts taught in this text, and I approve of it without reservation. This attitudinal recognition will make you a better police officer and a safer one. Every enlightened law officer should read this book and then live it."

—**Col. Hugh L. Mills Jr. (U.S. Army Ret.)**
Sheriff's Office
Jackson County, Missouri
Co-Author, Low Level Hell: A Scout Pilot in the Big Red One

"The authors offer a thorough assessment of the law enforcement community and the underlying problems that impede career excellence. Their provocative exploration into the human psyche encourages officers to more completely understand themselves, all the while providing empirical data that link this self-awareness to officer safety."

—**Kay White, MS, Forensic Psychology Associates**
Psychologist for the Kansas City Missouri Police Department

" … a courageous book that will, for those of us who courageously embrace its message, forever change the way we do police work for the better.… For those who have fallen into the trap of discouragement and cynicism, it will show us the way out of that darkness and renew our belief in the fact that we can make a difference if we care enough to change."

—**Brian McKenna**
Retired, Hazelwood Police Department, Missouri
Author of Officer Down! Lessons from the Streets
Owner of WINNING EDGE TRAINING in the St. Louis, Missouri area

"If law enforcement can move toward a model of unconditional respect, many of our problems will become much easier to manage: officers and citizens will be safer, community trust will grow, and our world will be a safer, saner place in which to live. I heartily recommend this book!"

—Steve Ashley, Use of Force Trainer and Risk Management Expert

"From the moment of reading the title of this book, I was hooked.… In a world where dignity and respect are sought-after commodities, it was refreshing to read such a thoughtful and scholarly discourse on how to give and receive those gifts."

—Susan Rockett
Chief of Public Safety
Mexico, Missouri
President of the National Association of Women Law Enforcement Executives

"Threefold strength of profound philosophical depth, practical hard-won experience, and professional integrity. May all those entrusted with the safety and welfare of the public be inspired and guided."

—Ivan Welch, Lieutenant Colonel, U.S. Army (Retired)

"This book and these principles hold the power to do more than transform law enforcement. These same principles hold tremendous value for success in the Boardroom or success in the War room."

—Frank J. Marsh
Deception Detection Instructor
Interview and Interrogation Instructor
Effective Communication Instructor
Success, Wellness, Attitude, and Teamwork Instructor

Unleashing the Power of Unconditional Respect

Transforming Law Enforcement and Police Training

Jack L. Colwell
Charles "Chip" Huth

CRC Press
Taylor & Francis Group
Boca Raton   London   New York

CRC Press is an imprint of the
Taylor & Francis Group, an **informa** business

Cover artwork by Zach Colwell.

CRC Press
Taylor & Francis Group
6000 Broken Sound Parkway NW, Suite 300
Boca Raton, FL 33487-2742

© 2010 by Taylor & Francis Group, LLC
CRC Press is an imprint of Taylor & Francis Group, an Informa business

No claim to original U.S. Government works

Printed in the United States of America on acid-free paper
Version Date: 20111012

International Standard Book Number: 978-1-4200-9974-4 (Hardback)

Library of Congress Cataloging-in-Publication Data

Colwell, Jack L.
   Unleashing the power of unconditional respect : transforming law enforcement and police training / Jack L. Colwell and Charles Huth.
      p. cm.
   Includes bibliographical references and index.
   ISBN 978-1-4200-9974-4
   1. Police training. 2. Police psychology. 3. Police-community relations. 4. Respect. I. Huth, Charles. II. Title.

HV7923.C578 2010
363.2'2--dc22   2009052533

Visit the Taylor & Francis Web site at
http://www.taylorandfrancis.com

and the CRC Press Web site at
http://www.crcpress.com

Table of Contents

Foreword

As a deception expert, I travel the world and willingly leave loved ones behind so that I might **serve** and possibly **save** law enforcement officers and agents from the dangers that await them. The greatest danger awaiting them has its origins in the thoughts and attitudes they choose to think. I have struggled trying to explain how their **success** and **survival** is directly related to the thoughts they choose to think about themselves and others. *Unleashing the Power of Unconditional Respect* by Jack Colwell and Charles Huth has succeeded where I have failed. This book and these principles hold the power to do more than transform law enforcement. These same principles hold tremendous value for success in the boardroom or success in the war room.

I offer more than my endorsement of this book. I emphatically state that any lasting positive change for the individual officer, agency, or society cannot occur until we all adopt the philosophy of "Unconditional Respect."

Adopting "Unconditional Respect" for the individual officer will improve his or her credibility and confidence on the street and in the office. Officers who embrace and understand "Unconditional Respect" will *improve* their performance, *improve* their safety, *improve* their effectiveness and at the same time reduce their stress and reduce the potential for complaints from the public against them.

Adopting "Unconditional Respect" for the agency holds the potential to *improve* organizational effectiveness, efficiency, morale, and communication. This approach will reduce court time, internal investigations, citizen complaints, and law suits and it will cost the agency and the individual almost nothing to implement. In these troubling times there is no greater return on investment then reading this book and embracing these principles.

Frank J. Marsh
Deception Detection Instructor
Interview and Interrogation Instructor
Effective Communication Instructor
Success, Wellness, Attitude, and Teamwork Instructor

Acknowledgments

Let me first acknowledge that with regard to anima, I have not remotely arrived and I never will. That is why social and structural support is so critical for each of us. So let me apologize for sometimes writing in an authoritative manner—as if I know all the answers. I deeply desire to help the men and women of law enforcement and the communities we serve, so my passion sometimes gets the best of me. I am a learner rather than an authority; I learn by studying timeless principles of truth, reading thoughtful people from various backgrounds, listening intently to all sorts of people to understand their perspective, thinking deeply about what is going on in our culture and world, and seeking wisdom. Please forgive my occasional vehemence in writing style and, rather, engage in these same learning processes as you read this book.

Next, thank you to the Kansas City, Missouri, Police Department. Over the last twenty-eight years, I have grown and matured greatly right along with this organization. Just as I have a long way to go in developing my own personal anima, so does this comparatively superior organization. Thanks to the KCPD for the opportunity to be one of the founders of its Leadership Academy and to interact with so many of you. I particularly need to thank my partner at the Leadership Academy, Dan Schmer, as he has labored with me, enduring my ceaseless stream of thoughts, ideas, initiatives, and concepts, and helped me hone them into curricula and processes. Thanks also to Randy Hopkins, James Thomas, and "Skip" Cox, who became role models of servant leadership and ones to clear the path—facilitating Dan and me in receiving top-tier training and excellent resources. Thanks to Ricky Smith, who originally loaned me a copy of *Courage: The Backbone of Leadership* by Diane and Gus Lee, especially because Ricky did so as both a supporter of the Leadership Academy and a courageous corrective to me (interestingly, we still disagree on the corrective). This book prompted me to assess my own integrity and courage, and allowed me to begin to understand the importance of unconditional respect. Thanks to Mark Hatcher, who originally helped me vet the tactical application of unconditional respect through a network of nationally recognized law enforcement defensive tactics instructors. Thanks to Frank Marsh with the National Drug Intelligence Center, who also allowed me to scrutinize the law enforcement application of unconditional respect with a group of experts in various related law enforcement fields. Thanks to the KCPD Psychologist, Kay White, who helped me think through these concepts and actualize some of them on the department.

From there, thanks to my friend Gary Hale, who happened to be visiting from Colorado and realized that he knew someone who knew my new favorite author. I wish to thank Gus and Diane Lee, who, through Gary's efforts, I am now honored to refer to as friends and mentors—and great supporters of this book and the goal it represents.

Finally, yet importantly from the KCPD, I wish to thank my coauthor, Chip Huth. He is the one who actualized the original paper I wrote on unconditional respect, giving the concept reality-based credibility. Chip also had the idea to make a proposal on a book. And from there, thanks to Carolyn Spence and the staff with Taylor & Francis Group, who took on two novices to write a potentially important and controversial book.

At home, I wish to thank my wife of almost three decades, Sherri, who also endured my endless stream of thoughts, ideas, and concepts. To her, and my children, who tolerated many, many hours of me reading, researching, thinking, and writing. To my mom and dad, who always assured me that the book would sell at least two copies. To my friends from various disciplines: Paul Mallory, Robert Carroll, Greg Dull (who also happens to be a captain on the KCPD), and many others, who also endured my ceaseless stream of ideas, patiently listening to, challenging, and honing my thinking. Toward the middle of the process, I began to have contact and learning opportunities at nearby Fort Leavenworth in Kansas. In so many ways, the noble warrior-scholars of the U.S. Army serve as a humbling reminder of what this book attempts to communicate.

Finally, and most importantly, thank you to my Lord and Savior Jesus Christ, who is the only true expression of integrity and courageous sacrificial love—and the ultimate answer to the dilemma of man posed in the opening of Chapter 1.

Jack Colwell

I would like to thank the men and women of law enforcement who faithfully serve our society each day. We intend this book to be a tool to serve those who serve others. I humbly submit that the concepts and ideas expressed in these pages are challenging. I personally struggle with them on a daily basis. This book does not purport to be a quick fix to organizational problems, but instead attempts to acknowledge the true nature of the challenges we face. Jack and I advocate an "inside-out" approach to overcoming these challenges. This approach begins with accepting personal responsibility for our inner way and our tendency to see the world in ways that make our mistreatment of others seem right.

I wish to thank all the servant leaders in our profession, both titled and untitled, for their selfless dedication to the ones they lead. Thank you to the men and women of the Kansas City, Missouri, Police Department. I have had the opportunity to teach people from agencies all across the globe, and I am convinced the officers of the KCPD are some of the most dedicated and professional public servants in the world. I would like to thank my coauthor, Jack, for his friendship and shining example of what it means to be a leader. I would like to thank my family for their constant encouragement. Lastly, I would like to thank my wife, Krista, for all the love and patience through the years. This project would not have been possible without your support.

Charles "Chip" Huth

We wish to express our appreciation to The Arbinger Institute, authors of *Leadership and Self-Deception* and *The Anatomy of Peace*. Arbinger's work about self-deception, self-betrayal, self-justification, way of being, seeing others as people rather than as objects, and helping things go right has been foundational for our understanding. We write about these Arbinger conceptions in this book with Arbinger's permission.

Introduction

"Leadership guru" Stephen Covey has noted a stunning finding from his research. Covey reported that the early material on leadership focused on character development as its basis. Then he noted that over time, the literature became personality focused: how to *look* good rather than *be* good.[1] In some ways the currents have begun to shift, but not before the world of business and politics colluded to give us the housing fund market collapse, and law enforcement has endured a drastic drop in credibility along with accompanying civil unrest and riots.

One residual of this trend is that most current law enforcement members have been taught a feigned or manufactured respect in dealing with each other and members of the public. Department members have been taught to "look" and "talk" in a respectful manner. The department member is allowed (if not encouraged) to entertain demeaning, prejudicial attitudes and have private conversations that are slanderous and defaming. It is assumed that as long as the publicly expressed words and behaviors (or that which are recorded on the video systems) are professional and efficient, all is fine. This book will begin to ask hard questions about the implications and effects of this type of training upon the culture of law enforcement and the communities they serve.

Most law enforcement organizational mission statements acknowledge the basic principle of Sir Robert Peel, founder of modern law enforcement: "Police must secure the willing co-operation of the public in voluntary observance of the law to be able to secure and maintain the respect of the public."[2] This premise is one of those principles that has become more relevant as time has passed and populations have grown. The math is simple: most police departments "police" a population that outnumbers their "on-duty" staff by thousands to one. If the vast majority of the public do not partner with the police in the mission of law enforcement, as in civil unrest or riots, the only possible outcomes are undesirable. One option is to capitulate and let criminals, such as rioters, wreak havoc. This was seen in the early stages of the Los Angeles riots of the early 1990s, which resulted in over fifty deaths, thousands

---

[1] Stephen R. Covey, The 7 Habits of Highly Effective People (New York: Fireside, 1989), 18–20.
[2] Robert Peel, "Sir Robert Peel's Nine Principles," http://nwpolice.org/peel.html (accessed July 22, 2008).

of injuries, and over $1 billion in property damage. The other option is to impose martial law. Either way, the public loses all respect for the police. They are seen as either a brutal occupying force or an irrelevant observer of chaos and suffering. The only logical alternative is that every contact with our communities should be viewed as an opportunity to build a partnership which supports a joint basic mission to foster safety, security, and prosperity. This requires a relentless striving for an anima rooted in integrity, buttressed by courage, and expressed in unconditional respect for all persons.

The Authors

Jack L. Colwell is the cofounder and co-instruc-
tor of the Regional Police Academy, Leadership
Academy for the Kansas City, Missouri, Police
Department, where he has served for twenty-eight
years. His duties have included patrol, tactical,
investigations, primary and secondary education,
and professional, leadership, and organizational
development. Jack holds numerous nationally
recognized leadership and personal development
content certifications. He is a recent graduate of
the U.S. Army's University of Foreign Military and
Cultural Studies (UFMCS, in Fort Leavenworth,
Kansas) Red Team Members Course 09-004. He
has created and implemented several successful training processes and ini-
tiatives. He is on the advisory board for the Vatterott College Criminal Justice
Program in St. Joseph, Missouri, and holds a bachelor of science degree from
the Baptist College of Florida. He resides in Kansas City, Missouri, with his
wife of twenty-nine years, Sherri. Sherri and Jack have five children, two of
whom are married (with one grandchild and another on the way). Blog: http://
unleashingrespect.blogspot.com; e-mail: unleashingrespect@gmail.com.

Charles "Chip" Huth is a national trainer and
vice president of the National Law Enforcement
Training Center. Chip is a sergeant with the Kansas
City, Missouri, Police Department (KCPD). He
has eighteen years of law enforcement experience.
He currently serves as a team leader for the Street
Crimes Unit Tactical Enforcement Squad, and has
coordinated and executed more than 1,200 high-
risk tactical operations. Chip is a certified national
trainer in defensive tactics, an expert witness in the
field of police operations and reasonable force, and
a subject matter expert on police use of force. He is
an adjunct instructor at the Leadership Academy
and a consultant for the KCPD's Office of General Counsel, the Missouri Peace
Officers Standards and Training Office, and the Missouri Attorney General's

Office. He is a member of the International Law Enforcement Educators and Trainers Association and the National Tactical Officers Association. Chip has thirty years of experience in the martial arts, with a background in competitive judo and kickboxing. He is a veteran of the U.S. Army and lives in Kansas City, Missouri, with his wife, Krista, and his two sons. Blog: http:// unleashingrespect.blogspot.com; e-mail: unleashingrespect@gmail.com.

A Thin Blue Line Through the Heart of Every Cop

1

"The *Ordenienst*, or Jewish police in Westerbork, were universally detested by camp inmates for their cruelty and role in collaborating with the Nazis."[*]

The photo that accompanies this quote on the website is bone chilling. It shows a formation of uniformed Jewish police marching with great vigor, sporting their badges with a blackened incinerator stack in the background. Indeed as Aldous Huxley so aptly said, "Cynical realism is the intelligent man's best excuse for doing nothing in an intolerable situation."

Therefore:

> The profession of law enforcement
> requires a relentless striving for a personal anima
> (inner way) which sees others as people
> and is rooted in integrity, buttressed by courage,
> and expressed as unconditional respect for all.

It takes only a cursory reading of history, or the daily newspaper, to conclude that humans hold a unique status. They can be the most dangerous, selfish, cruel, and unpredictable—and the most trustworthy, altruistic, kind, and dependable—of creatures. Even more perplexing is that the same individual will occasionally make headlines as being polar opposites from the perspective of his victims versus that of his family and friends: for example, there was a family man and pharmacist who diluted cancer drugs for unseemly profit and used the income to support his church's building fund.[†] Also consider the "former church congregation president and Boy Scout leader" who was simultaneously the infamously horrid BTK (bind torture kill) serial killer.[‡] On Christmas Eve 2008, a recently divorced man with "no criminal record and no history of violence" who "also served regularly as an usher at evening Mass at Holy Redeemer Catholic Church in Montrose [California]" went to his former-in laws' house dressed in a Santa

---

[*] "Jewish Police in Westerbork," in *A Teacher's Guide to the Holocaust.* http://fcit.usf.edu/HOLOCAUST/gallery/11548.HTM (accessed February 25, 2010).

[†] "Drug-Diluting Pharmacist Gets 30 Years: Judge Calls Druggist's Crime 'a Shock to the Civilized Conscience,'" CBSNews.com, December 5, 2002, http://www.cbsnews.com/stories/2002/02/25/national/main330499.shtml (accessed June 13, 2008).

[‡] Sam Coates, "Rader Gets 175 Years For BTK Slayings Killer: 'I Hope Someday God Will Accept Me,'Washington Post, August 19, 2005, p. A03, http://www.washingtonpost.com/wp-dyn/content/article/2005/08/18/AR2005081800201.html.

suit complete with "presents." When an eight-year-old girl opened the door for "Santa," he opened a "present" and shot the little girl in the face with a handgun. He then went on a shooting spree, indiscriminately targeting the partygoers, killing nine, and injuring others. He then opened another "present," revealing a device that sprayed a pressurized flammable liquid. After setting the house ablaze, he went to his brother's house, where later he apparently shot himself to death. Neighbors were shocked, and one described him as "the nicest guy you could imagine. Always a pleasure to talk to, always a big smile."[*]

Enter into this reality the everyday heroes we know as police officers. These men and women deal daily with the most dangerous and unpredictable people our current civilization has to offer. Conversely, for law enforcement efforts to be successful, the officer is to inspire community trust and support with every citizen contact.

We humbly submit that there is one "anima" that allows officers to operate safely and effectively when dealing across the broad spectrum of humanity's extremes. *Anima* is a fascinating word that is uniquely suited to explain this concept. The etymology of it has references to the true inner self, or the psyche, as opposed to a persona or professional face. One historical use of the word refers to a type of personal body armor used in the sixteenth century similar to that worn by the Roman legions. Apparently the word *anima* was used because it was worn directly over the vital areas of the body rather than held away as a shield. So, for the purpose of this book we are advocating a personal anima: an inner self that is particularly suited for, as Plato's *Republic* held, the noble guardians of our communities. Thankfully, most people will never know the challenges our noble guardians face and deal with on a daily basis. Most people will never *really* understand why an "inner shield" is the only hope of protecting the hearts and minds of our noble guardians from cynicism and apathy. Nevertheless, the guardians reading this do, and to you we humbly salute your brave, selfless service. We commend this writing to you as both; painfully realistic and blunt, and yet hopefully insightful look at the intense pressure that relentlessly bears down upon those in our profession. This ignoble pressure exudes both from the inside of our profession and from the outside upon our profession. Like a doctor digging for a biopsy of a deadly cancer, the diagnosis can be as painful as the cure, and for that we humbly express regret.

This idea is not a behavior theory; it is simply a way of illustrating the internal "inner way" that we are proposing. We are primarily using the word anima to draw attention to the fact this concept is different. For decades,

---

[*] Christina Hoag, "Man in Santa Suit Kills 8, Self on Christmas Eve," Associated Press, December 26, 2008, http://news.yahoo.com/s/ap/20081226/ap_on_re_us/santa_shooting (accessed December 26, 2008).

law enforcement has been taught to interact with the public with a tactical face, or persona. Our advocated anima is rooted in personal integrity and buttressed by courage. It manifests itself as unconditional respect for all people. The parallel to personal body armor is easily made because it protects the noble guardian—emotionally, mentally, socially, and tactically.* This proposed anima not only enhances personal safety at work but also is equally effective on- or off-duty. With this anima, there is no need for officers to attempt to develop multiple perceptual sets in order to maneuver the spectrum of humanity and social situations and still maintain officer safety. Kevin M. Gilmartin, Ph.D., who is considered by many to be one of the preeminent authorities on police stress and emotional survival, conjectures that a perceptual state he calls "hypervigilance" is the source of many of the psychological and sociological woes of law enforcement officers. This perceptual state regards everything at work as potentially life-threatening. It causes a mild state of stimulation during the entire shift and sends the officer home wholly exhausted and increasingly unable to socialize with nonpolice. Gilmartin encourages officers to practice perceptual states other than hypervigilance when off-duty.† As previously stated, and as will be elaborated on at length in this book, the anima we are advocating and the resulting unconditional respect provide a perceptual set for officer safety at work and are readily transferable to any social environment.

This anima is a simple concept but at the same time requires the most rigorous and relentless personal discipline to internalize and actualize. Why? Because the honorable men and women of law enforcement who pursue this anima (the authors included) are simultaneously members of the same humanity who, not unlike those cited in the following examples, are subject to manipulation by the social context in which they find themselves. For a sobering look at our "human potential," consider those who in a matter of days went from "average" people with a wholesome trade to being part of mass execution under the Nazi regime—an example we'll come back to in Chapter 1. Consider the overwhelming majority of German citizens who gave tacit approval to such actions. *Washington Post* columnist Richard Cohen reflects on this reality in his review of the bone-chilling movie *Downfall* that deals with the last days of Adolf Hitler in his underground bunker. Comparing

---

* S.v. "Anima," Dictionary.com, WordNet® 3.0, Princeton University, http://dictionary. reference.com/browse/anima (accessed July 25, 2008); and s.v. "Anima," Reference.com, Wikipedia, http://www.reference.com/browse/wiki/Anima (accessed July 25, 2008). See also http://southtowerarmouringguild.blogspot.com/2007/11/anima-armour.html. We are not speaking of anima in the Jungian sense of the word, simply the "inner self" concept.
† Kevin Gilmartin, Ph.D., "Hypervigilance: A Learned Perceptual Set and Its Consequences on Police Stress," http://emotionalsurvival.com/hypervigilance.htm (accessed September 4, 2009).

the humanity and evil of Hitler with the willingness of the German people to follow and assist him and then in an unbelievably short time become a solid democratic society, Cohen says this:

> [A] whole people's madness is a different story.... This quality of the Germans during the Third Reich, this quality of the Chinese during Mao's Great Leap Forward, this quality of the Cambodians or the Rwandans or—in 1937–38— the Japanese in Nanking, resides in us all.*

Reflect on the ethnic cleansing in mid-1994 Rwanda, where up to a million Rwandans were slaughtered by fellow countrymen who happened to be of a different ethnic background. A terrifying account was captured by Immaculée Ilibagiza, who survived the genocide by hiding in a small bathroom for several months. In her book, Ilibagiza recounts hearing the hoard charging through the house of a pastor who had provided refuge. They were hunting her down, intending to hack her to death with machetes and spears. At one point, she could distinctly hear the voice of a "family friend" referring to her as one more of hundreds of "cockroaches" he had crushed.†

Contemplate the account of Yehiel Dinur, a concentration camp survivor who was present to testify at the trial of Adolf Eichmann, sometimes referred to as the architect of the Nazi holocaust. Shortly after seeing Eichmann for the first time, Dinur was so overcome that he fainted. Later, when interviewed about why he was so overwhelmed that he lost consciousness, Dinur said that it was because Eichmann was not the monster he expected, but because Eichmann was so terribly normal. Dinur saw himself in Eichmann, and that is what overwhelmed him.‡

While the social context and circumstances never eliminate personal responsibility, consider the stance recorded in *APA Online*, the American Psychological Association's online journal, by an expert witness in the Abu Ghraib prison scandal:

> That line between good and evil is permeable.... Any of us can move across it.... I argue that we all have the capacity for love and evil—to be Mother Theresa, to be Hitler or Saddam Hussein. It's the situation that brings that out.§

---

* Richard Cohen, "Evil's Willing Followers" Washington Post, April 26, 2005, http://www.washingtonpost.com/wp-dyn/content/article/2005/04/25/AR2005042501347.html (accessed August 1, 2009).

† Immaculée Ilibagiza, Left To Tell: Discovering God amidst the Rwandan Holocaust (Carlsbad, Calif.: Hay House, 2007).

‡ This account was reported by Charles Colson in his book Who Speaks for God: Determining the Value System You Will Live By (Carol Stream, Ill.: Tyndale House, 1994).

§ Melissa Dittman, "What Makes Good People Do Bad Things?" APA Online: Monitor on Psychology 35, no. 9 (October 2004): http://www.apa.org/monitor/oct04/goodbad.html. In this article, former APA president Philip Zimbardo drew from research to help explain evil under the backdrop of recent Iraqi prisoner abuses at Abu Ghraib.

In stark distinction, this "anima" that we are recommending is rooted in integrity and necessarily requires the courage to act for what is right regardless of risk to self in the prevailing social context. This kind of anima gives humanity people like Dietrich Bonheoffer, the Christian pastor who refused to cooperate with the Nazis, even though he would inevitably be imprisoned and executed. This kind of anima also produces people like Mahatma Gandhi, Nelson Mandela, and Martin Luther King—people who stand against the overwhelming social tide of evil that often sweeps humanity. Sometimes they lead a revolution of good to transform a culture, sometimes they die alone at the hands of an executioner, but their legacies nonetheless echo down through history, inspiring others on. To that end, this anima we are advocating not only leaves the officer safer and more effective, but also acts to provide constructive social influence, or even inspiration. We do not claim to have "arrived"; rather, we invite others to join us in the most difficult process of personal development, accountability, and responsibility we have ever attempted.

In this book two radically different paths will be laid before the reader. One is the well-worn and traveled path of the masses, allowing oneself to be permeated and controlled by the dictates of the prevailing social pressures and cultural mind-sets. The other approach is of personal anima: that sees all people as people, is rooted in integrity, reinforced by courage, and expressed through unconditional respect for all.

Building personal anima begins with some simple but startlingly profound realizations and building accountability systems around them. These new structures can be quantified by the following points:

- I am a human being, endowed with the gift of self-examination. In other words, I have a conscience and am therefore responsible for my thoughts, words, actions, and inactions.
- I am *not* a simple stimulus–response mechanism. I cannot simply blame others for my reactions and responses.
- I must face the fact that I have prejudices, loyalties, desires, and fears that cloud my judgment and shroud me in self-deception. Said another way, when I am wrong I will almost certainly deceive myself with self-justification and blame directed at other people and circumstances—I will naturally assume I am right at my most wrong points.

In this book we intend to demonstrate that this anima is desperately needed in law enforcement and will provide the foundation for the physical, psychological, sociological, and tactical benefits of *Unleashing the Power of Unconditional Respect*.

To this end, this chapter will discuss why courage is lacking in a bravery-rich culture such as law enforcement. The second chapter will demonstrate how personal integrity is the foundation for unconditional respect, and reasons why having and maintaining integrity are some of the most difficult struggles in an individual's life. Chapter 3 will enumerate some of the tactical benefits of unconditional respect. Chapters 4 through 6 will look at the interpersonal benefits of unconditional respect, with Chapter 5 specifically focusing in on anima-based leadership core competencies. Chapter 7 will deal with how unconditional respect affects law enforcement's interaction with the communities in which it operates. Chapter 8 will explain how unconditional respect creates and builds high character. Finally, Chapter 9 will deal with influencing an organizational culture toward unconditional respect.

Land of the Free and Home of the Brave—but Where are the Courageous?

Quietly, after a leadership academy class, a lone officer approaches the instructor and says something like this: "I was about ready to give it up, to quit. I grew up in an ethnic area of our city. It is the home of my family. I came on the PD so that I could serve this community that I love so much. It's painful to hear other members slam my community in front of me, as if I am not there, or they assume that since I wear the badge I am as cynical and disrespectful as they are about the people of this community. But now that I have seen that the leadership academy is teaching unconditional respect, that it will increasingly become part of the culture of this organization, I am encouraged. I can hope once again. Thank you."

My reply to him: "No, officer—thank you!"

Courage: Dead on Arrival

Social researchers and philosophical observers have generally realized that the most basic human instinct for survival has at its core the need to be socially connected. Historically, extrication from the social group meant death not only for the individual but also for the individual's family and progeny, and even for the "social contract" itself.

Socrates, to give an example from western philosophy, was said to uphold the value of the social contract literally to his death by a self-inflicted execution. Socrates chose to drink poison rather than dishonor the social contract of the community, even though a way of escape had been arranged. The great philosopher reportedly believed that once a person lives under a civil, social system, he or she is bound to it by a sense of honor, even in the face of injustice.[*]

---

[*] Plato, Crito, written 360 B.C.E., trans. Benjamin Jowett. http://classics.mit.edu/Plato/crito.html. Socrates' death is a complex issue. He died the death of a courageous hero in order to teach his core moral belief; "It is worse to do wrong than to suffer wrong." He died in obedience to the laws of Athens. Therefore, his death can be seen as upholding the social contract.

A prevalent philosophy from southern Africa, where relationships and social allegiances are central, is called the "spirit of ubuntu." To understand this philosophy, one must understand some of its terms. The greeting *SawaBona* means "I see you," and is the equivalent of "hello" in English. The response, *Sikhona*, would be translated as "I am here." In other words, until you see and acknowledge me, I am not here. When you see me, you bring me into existence. "The whole philosophy of 'Umuntu ngumuntu abantu[,]' a person is a person because of other people, hinges on this. There is no conception of life outside the other."* From the Near East is the biblical account of one who violated the social contract:

> And ... all Israel ... took Achan ... and his sons, and his daughters.... And all Israel stoned him with stones, and burned them with fire, after they had stoned them with stones. And they raised over him a great heap of stones unto this day.[†]

And from some Far East traditions, Gus Lee explains how the "greatest fear was being *kong hsu*, socially disconnected and abandoned by the *jia*, the clan."[‡]

What these examples all show is that at our core, all humanity evidences that a fear of being ostracized from the group or clan is a fate worse than death; indeed, it may represent the closest thing to "eternal death" that a secular mind is willing to consider. As a result, some of history's most notable acts of bravery represent a deep desire to maintain and protect one's standing in, and defense of, the social context with which they identify. Therefore, absent an anima of stalwart personal integrity, and the courage to stand alone against the social tide, the social context one identifies with generally becomes the determining factor in values and norms.

The integrity and courage it takes for an individual to stand alone against the pressure of one's own social grouping are rare commodities in humanity. This fact is a particularly virulent problem because when people choose to draw their sense of right and wrong from their social grouping (consider the citizens who facilitated the slaughter of millions in Nazi Germany, Stalin's Russia, or Communist China), they are self-deceived about their morality. At the same time, they are blind to their own self-deception because it comes wrapped in self-justification and an internal dialogue of condemning and blaming others.

---

* Thembayona Paulus Emmanuel Manci, The Response of African Religion to Poverty, with Specific Reference to the Umzimkhulu Municipality, http://etd.unisa.ac.za/ ETD-db/theses/available/etd-01302006-152512/unrestricted/01thesis.pdf (accessed September 5, 2009).

† Joshua 7:24–26, King James Version, http://bibleresources.bible.com/passagesearchresults2. php?passage1=Joshua+7&book_id=6&version1=9&tp=24&c=7 (accessed September 4, 2009).

‡ Gus Lee, Courage: The Backbone of Leadership (San Francisco: Jossey-Bass, 2006), 39.

This thesis has been clearly argued by C. Terry Warner, who summarizes that humans "systematically keep ourselves from understanding ourselves" by "going against our honest feelings about what's right and wrong for us to do."* This self-deception is always acted out in their interactions with the social and structural systems that surround them. The effects of this reality were shockingly (pun intended) demonstrated by Dr. Stanley Milgram at Yale University in 1961–1962. Random people were easily persuaded to deliver seemingly painful or fatal jolts of electricity to another person they had just met. Many of the "executioners" later expressed a sense of pride in having been efficient at completing the experiment.

> Stark authority was pitted against the subjects' strongest moral imperatives against hurting others, and, with the subjects' ears ringing with the screams of the victims, authority won more often than not.[†]

Milgram's work disturbingly supported the much-maligned postulations of Hannah Arendt, a twentieth-century political philosopher. Arendt argued in her work *Eichmann in Jerusalem: A Report on the Banality of Evil* that Nazi leader Adolf Eichmann and the executioners of the death camps were not monstrous oddities of humankind. Rather, they were unnervingly normal people working out of the values of loyalty and obedience. Eichmann and his cohorts simply worked within a social system that precipitated disconnection between their sense of moral awareness and responsibility and the heinous atrocities they dutifully carried out.

> Arendt concluded … Eichmann was an utterly innocuous individual. He operated unthinkingly, following orders, efficiently carrying them out, with no consideration of their effects upon those he targeted. The … extermination of the Jews became indistinguishable from any other bureaucratically assigned and discharged responsibility for Eichmann and his cohorts.[‡]

Consider next the Ford Motor Company which dealt with the ethical dilemma of the Pinto in 1971. Reports indicate that during *pre-production*, crash test engineers found that during relatively low-speed rear-impact collisions (about 30 mph), the gas tank would rupture, discharging gas, and the doors would jam closed. This would obviously create a nightmarish

---

* C. Terry Warner, "What We Are," © 1986, 1999 C. Terry Warner, all rights reserved, http://www.arbinger.com/downloads/what_we_are.pdf (accessed July 22, 2008). Dr. C. Terry Warner is chair of the Philosophy Department at Brigham Young University and one of the founders of the Arbinger Institute.

† "The Perils of Obedience," Harper's Magazine, abridged and adapted from Stanley Milgram, Obedience to Authority, © 1974 by Stanley Milgram, http://www.age-of-the-sage.org/psychology/milgram_perils_authority_1974.html (accessed August 2, 2008).

‡ Majid Yar, "Hannah Arendt (1906–1975): Chronology of Life and Works," 2006, http://www.iep.utm.edu/a/arendt.htm#H6 (accessed August 2, 2008). At the time, some strongly reacted to her writings, but her work has become considered very credible.

situation. The occupants would be trapped in a burning car and suffer a horrible death. Ford, however, was under social and economic pressure to get the car into production. It was also looking through the sterile coldness of "cost-benefit analysis," and as a result the Pinto went into production without the needed modifications.* One picture is worth a thousand words on a spreadsheet about the horror that fell upon the unsuspecting Pinto occupants in the last few moments of their lives following a rear-end collision.

Another university study tried to explain how easily humans will bend even moral rules that they know are important. People in the study were willing to pass by rather than stop and render aid to people in an emergency because the participants pictured themselves in a hurry with a group of people already waiting for them elsewhere. The social obligation to avoid being late overrode their obligation of personal integrity to stop and help. What made the study poignant was that the people in a hurry were on their way to *teach the group* about the classic biblical account of the "Good Samaritan," who is a model of helping others in need.†

John Reid, a Chicago detective in the 1940s, harnessed the innateness and power of self-deception and built a world-renowned interrogation process around it. According to Reid, the key element in obtaining a confession from a guilty subject is to develop a theme that blames someone else:

> [P]lace the moral blame for his actions on some other person or some outside set of circumstances. This procedure is founded on a very basic aspect of human nature—most people tend to minimize their responsibility for their actions by placing blame upon someone or something else.‡

To summarize this reality with an analogy, to have the courage to stand alone against social tides, integrity (to discern right from wrong regardless of personal biases, fears, loyalties, and prejudice) is like oxygen. Integrity breathes life into dead courage (to act for what is right regardless of personal danger when members of my social grouping do not agree with the act).

---

* Mark Dowie, "Pinto Madness," Mother Jones, http://www.motherjones.com/politics/1977/09/pinto-madness (accessed August 8, 2009); and Anonymous, "Profits before People," Canada and the World Backgrounder, May 1, 2003, http://elibrary.bigchalk.com.proxy.mcpl.lib.mo.us/libweb/elib/do/document?set=search&groupid=1&requestid=lib_standard&resultid=1&edition=&ts=02BFEFF55FB6DA58523FE554588D5BCF_1221995789393&start=1&urn=urn%3Abigchalk%3AUS%3BBCLib%3Bdocument%3B7 5236710 (accessed September 21, 2008).

† J. M. Darley and C. D. Batson, "'From Jerusalem to Jericho': A Study of Situational and Dispositional Variables in Helping Behavior," JPSP 27 (1973): 100–8, http://faculty.babson.edu/krollag/org_site/soc_psych/darley_samarit.html (accessed July 22, 2008). The Good Samaritan appears in Luke 10:25–37, King James Version.

‡ "The Reid Technique," http://www.reid.com/educational_info/critictechnique.html (accessed July 21, 2008).

String of Perils

The "string" that supports each of these perils and allows tasks to link
to catastrophe is **self deception:**
*Blinding presuppositions and schemas, that are fortified with personal
justifications and / or blame directed at others. Left unchallenged self
deception becomes mindless (not safe to discuss or disagree) groupthink.*

Remove the **string** and the ***entire error chain evaporates.***
None of the links stand, no error chain exists.
Mitigation tactics should be directed at identifying and mitigating each
individual peril BUT primary effort should always be directed at eliminating
the "string" that all the perils ride upon.

**The only way to effectively interact with the "String of Perils" is to first
assume "*My* self deception is the string."**

Figure 1.1

Self-deception is like carbon monoxide (CO); it is the opposite of integrity,
and it kills courage. The insidious problem with carbon monoxide poisoning
is that the victim will typically blame the symptoms (nausea, vomiting) on
something else, like a flu bug or a bad enchilada. The victim will then "sleep
it off" in the very environment that is killing her. Similarly, the insidious
problem with self-deception is that the victim will blame the symptoms (apathy, cynicism, broken relationships, rampant gossip and rumormongering,
ineffective communication, no accountability) on everyone and everything
else. The victim then "sleeps it off" in the very self-deception, that is destroy-
ing him psychologically, emotionally, and socially. See the "string of perils"
illustration (Figure 1.1) for a visualization of the relationship between *problematic symptoms* and self-deception.

Reviving Courage: Root It in Personal Integrity, and Distinguish It from Bravery

Historically, bravery and valor were synonymous: both represented *physical
action* toward what is right at risk to self. Courage has been seen as involving moral action toward what is right. What if one drew another distinction between courage and bravery? What if bravery came to be known this
way? Bravery is acting for what is right, regardless of personal risk, when the
actors' *perceived social grouping believes in and agrees with them.*

A lone officer entering a building to confront a well-armed "active shooter" who is slaughtering innocent people is performing an act of extreme bravery. Everyone knows it, and everyone applauds.

We are advocating making a distinct differentiation with courage: acting for what is right, regardless of personal risk, when the actors' *perceived social grouping does not agree*.

Courage in Action versus Courage: Dead on Arrival

An officer finds himself in a conversation among several peers that suddenly turns to how worthless and trashy a particular ethnic group is. What's more, his peers agree that the area of the city where this group primarily resides should just be "napalmed" to solve the agency's worst problems. Standing for the dignity and value of the ethnic group would be an act of courage. The officer would inevitably face social alienation, which would likely become an officer safety issue. While standing on enduring principles of right and wrong can be costly in the short run, it will be beneficial to all in the long run.

Consider, for example, those known as whistleblowers. These are people who breach silos of *omerta* (a term popularized by organized crime referring to a code of silence) and point out unscrupulous and dangerous behaviors of business and government. In the short term, they are unpopular, maligned, demoted, and even fired. This is because social structures, including workplaces, naturally tend to value loyalty over integrity. However, in the long run they bring a constant sense of accountability and transparency to organizations and administrations that have lost their integrity and social conscience. Whistleblowers ensure a safe workplace and community along with a hedge against the tyranny of oppressive government.*

A young civilian desk clerk in a private conversation suddenly bristles as if an electric shock ran up her spine. Then, in hushed tones, she says that when the phone rings and the caller ID indicates the call is coming from a particular division within the agency, she gets a sick feeling in her gut. Experience tells her that the person on the other end will likely be angry, rude, and abrasive. She wonders out loud how citizens who call that zone must be treated if other department employees are treated this way. What leads to an entire division getting a reputation as rude and abrasive? Occasionally, individual division commanders live out their command being viewed as a social terrorist spreading hostility and cynicism through the rank and file as well as

---

* Charles S. Clark, "Whistleblowers," The CQ Researcher, published by Congressional Quarterly, http://library.cqpress.com.proxy.mcpl.lib.mo.us/cqresearcher/getpdf.php?file=cqr19971205.pdf (accessed September 21, 2008).

the community they "serve," like an epidemic. (refer again to the "string of perils" (Figure 1.1) simply insert different perils.

This hypothetical commander is no different from anyone reading this book—or those of us writing this book, for that matter. They are resting fine in the "carbon monoxide (CO) poisoning" of self-deception; beyond that, their problem is twofold:

- They work in an organization where conflict avoidance (cowardice) is the social norm and no systems are in place to promote courage, that is, to "en-courage" members to act for what is right.
- Given the conflict-avoidant culture, no one in their circle of acquaintances has the stalwart personal integrity and courage (anima) to treat them with the most basic form of respect. To a person, those around them have refused to stand on enduring principles of right and wrong. They have neither given the commander the genuine, relevant, respectful feedback that everyone but him (deep in the CO poisoning of self-deception) knows he needs, nor have they held the commander accountable for his actions and results. (another "string of perils")

At the same time, the decision to not provide relevant, respectful feedback or hold others accountable is so immersed in self-justifying and others-condemning internal dialogue that the option of giving relevant feedback is not even consciously considered. Rather, if anyone eventually acts, it is only after their anger and frustration have reached the boiling point. They spew over in a fit of rage, spitting out venomous words that are neither respectful nor relevant. They make their own behavior a spectacle that eclipses and justifies the behavior of the one who originally needed the feedback. The "insubordinate hothead" is summarily disciplined and given the most undesirable assignment that can be found (still another string of perils). As a result, the cultural downward spiral into cynicism, brooding hostility, and apathy with no accountability continues.

Supporting Courage: Establish Systems Support and Build Social Foundations

Famed police corruption–fighting figure Frank Serpico appeared before the New York City Council in 1997 and gave the same message he gave twenty-six years earlier as a "whistleblower" of police corruption (Serpico prefers the term lamplighter rather than whistleblower). Serpico argued that the social systems that support the "blue wall of silence" reach from top to bottom in policing. He explained that good role models are needed at the very top of police organizations. When top brass compromise personal and organizational integrity and are not held accountable, it is little wonder that millions of dollars are paid out in brutality cases for actions taken at the line level.

> Serpico urged the council to pierce the "blue wall of silence" by rewarding honest officers. "I said this to the Knapp Commission over 25 years ago," Serpico said. "We must create an atmosphere where the crooked cop fears the honest cop, and not the other way around."*

You will recall from the earlier chapter preview that the final chapter in this book will deal with practical ways to influence an organizational culture toward integrity, courage, and unconditional respect for all. For now, it suffices to say that because of the natural disposition of humans to unwittingly walk in lockstep with the social and structural systems they identify with, stated organizational values must be clearly rooted in high core values such as integrity, courage, and character.[†] Operational values (the values that are actually acted out) must be aligned from top to bottom with stated values. Policies and social interaction (what happens to those who act for what is right) must support the stated values. Investments must continuously be made to develop and support the anima of individual members.

Law enforcement agencies have historically encouraged and instilled bravery, which is good. It is time to begin to encourage and instill courage rooted in integrity. This would begin to break down the personal deception of individuals, and the corresponding "blue wall of silence" that emanates from it. When courageous, relevant, respectful communication becomes normative in the police culture, it will produce true accountability around enduring principles of right and wrong at all levels of police organizations. This would inspire the trust of the members and citizens, unleashing their natural talents and creative energy around the basic mission of law enforcement. In time, this would produce greatness in organizations and synergistic productivity with their communities. This is evident in that, just as we previously considered how social influence structures (e.g., the Nazis or the Communist Revolution) can lead to wholesale evil behavior, the opposite can also be true. Unleashing the power of personal anima, rooted in integrity and expressed in unconditional respect for all, will have tremendous positive results.

Now we turn our attention to how one stands against the social tide within an organization and finds the courage to be genuinely respectful to all others regardless of social risk.

---

* Peg Tyre, "Serpico Resurrects His Decades-Old Criticism of NYPD," Reuters, 1997, http://www.cnn.com/US/9709/23/serpico.brutality/index.html#cases (accessed August 2, 2008).
† Lee, Courage.

Integrity
The Basis of
Unconditional Respect

2

At first glance, the deep desire to protect one's social standing may not seem like much of an obstacle to integrity, but that is a dangerous assumption. This single issue, manifest in multiple ways, is arguably the source of most, if not all, of the destructive prejudices and contemptuous or apathetic attitudes that haunt law enforcement organizations today. One humorous, folkloric way of describing this phenomenon is affectionately known as the "inverted asshole theory":

> When I first came on, I quickly realized what assholes those I deal with and arrest every day are. They are stupid, loud, trashy, and smelly. As I talk to my old (non-L.E.) buddies about what a rush it is to kick these idiots' asses, I realize that my old buddies don't get it; in fact, they are assholes, too. After I received a few complaints from citizens who heard me telling and showing an arrestee what an asshole he is, I realized that anyone who is not law enforcement is an asshole. Then some of the commanders started getting in my ass about all the complaints I was getting from these assholes, so now I know that the commanders are assholes too. These idiots that ride this sector on the other watches never carry their own weight and don't take care of the equipment, even though they have nothing else to do. What a bunch of assholes! The other sectors on my watch are not covering their own sector, and they dodge report calls; what assholes! It has finally dawned on me that everyone is an asshole but my partner; I am suspicious of him, but I don't tell him. I do tell all the other assholes I am surrounded by, though, because after all, it takes one to know one.*

What this vernacular looks like in more professional language has been systematically captured by the Arbinger Institute in *The Anatomy of Peace: Resolving the Heart of Conflict.*† Arbinger calls this form of self-betrayal the "Better-Than Box." The self-betrayer views herself as superior, important, virtuous, and right. She views others as inferior, incapable, irrelevant, false, and

---

* This theoretical construct (or many variations of it) of police perception has wide circulation and is generally understood to be a humorous hyperbolic explanation of internal realities. This theory could be considered folklore; the authors have no idea as to the source.
† Arbinger Institute, The Anatomy of Peace: Resolving the Heart of Conflict (San Francisco: Barrett-Koehler, 2008), 107, 108.

wrong. As a result, she has feelings of impatience, disdain, and indifference and views the world as competitive, troubled, and needy of her. Interestingly, in the New Testament people with this persona were typified by a sect known as the Pharisees. They saw themselves as morally superior (Luke 18:9–12) and despised Jesus because He had regard for the morally inferior (Luke 15:1–2). One can read Matthew 23 for Jesus' commentary on the Pharisees.

To illustrate how this self-deception works, imagine asking a room full of law enforcement commanders a rhetorical question: "You are newly promoted and are running late to your first command staff meeting; is it OK to speed?" This question comes across as something a psychotic individual would ask. It does not even make sense; it does not compute. Generally, law enforcement is so immersed in a self-justifying social context (in this case, that it's OK for *them* to speed whenever they want) that this question sadly sounds like someone is muttering in a foreign language. Now ask the commanders another rhetorical question: "You are a teenager attending a rough inner-city school. Your father, who you have never met, is in prison, and your mother is an addict and a prostitute. You live in fear of bullying and brutality every day. You have never experienced anything but hostility and contempt from the police. Is it OK to join a gang for self-preservation and feel rage toward the police commander who goes speeding by because you see him as the ultimate hypocrite?"

Arbinger does a great job of demonstrating what the New Testament stated, Arendt postulated, Milgram verified, and John Reid developed. When one person treats another as a "less than human object," the human mind has an automatic proclivity to self-justify. As we self-justify, we become increasingly frustrated and angry with others as we amplify and stereotype their weaknesses and faults.

This tenet is why it is impossible to have an internal attitude of unconditional respect for others without a stalwart inner integrity that is buttressed by courage. C. S. Lewis explained this succinctly: "Courage is not simply one of the virtues but the form of every virtue at the testing point."* If people draw their values from social norms rather than a stalwart inner integrity (e.g., it's OK for police to speed):

- They will automatically feel threatened by and have disdain toward others who draw their values from different social norms (e.g., those who believe it's OK to join a gang and hate the police).
- They will lose the ability to have unconditional respect for others (i.e., see them and treat them as humans) and will blame others for the contempt they feel toward them.

---

* Quotes in Lee, Courage, 11.

- They will automatically be blinded to the deteriorating social values in which they are immersed.
- They will lack the courage to stand on enduring principles of right and wrong against the social tide.

One disturbing note that captures the natural and social consequences of allowing self-deception (the opposite of personal integrity) and disingenuous social identification to grow into a poisonous social mushroom cloud is the aforementioned *omerta* or blue wall of silence. One of the most startling cases in recent history was the now-infamous account of a Haitian immigrant, Abner Louima, who in 1997 was beaten and sodomized with a wooden rod while handcuffed in the custody of the New York Police Department (NYPD). The most disturbing part of this story is that the blue wall of silence (or silo of omerta) held for almost two years, all the way into the trial. Reports indicated many officers observed the brutality and did not intervene:

> [A]t the time of the assault the officer bragged to other officers about "how he broke a man down." "He actually went and retrieved the stick with Mr. Louima's feces still on it and walked around the precinct, brandishing this feces-filled stick in front of his fellow police officers."*

The above account succinctly and sadly captures the natural consequences of allowing a culture of rampant internal self-deception and external condemnation along with no accountability. (Refer to the string of perils, Figure 1.1, simply insert different perils.) Conversely, when individuals have the integrity to identify right from wrong and not get swept up in a social tide of self-justification, self-righteousness, and contempt toward others, the desire to see and treat others as human beings surfaces in their character. This desire is expressed as unconditional respect for all people and the courage to confront those who treat others with disdain. For those with high levels of personal anima, one question ruminates through conscious and subconscious thought: "What is right?" As these individuals with high moral character begin to act for what is right, slowly the culture begins to shift. Others with little or no personal anima who see a culture of integrity emerging around them are confronted, perhaps for the first time, by their own internal sense of right and wrong—their conscience. They begin to ask three questions: what is right (do I have the integrity)? Is acting for what is right worth it (do I have the courage)? Can I do it (do I have the skills)?

---

* "30-Year Sentence for N.Y. Policeman in Torture of Black Man," CNN.com, December 13, 1999, http://archives.cnn.com/1999/US/12/13/volpe.sentencing.02/index.html (accessed July 22, 2008).

Rule of 30

To illustrate this concept, I have created an imaginary scale from zero to thirty rating personal integrity, courage, and the skills to act for what is right in any particular situation (Point of Integrity). At the highest level (of thirty), an individual will always act for what is right regardless of social pressures and personal risks and will have the skills to do so (e.g., Frank Serpico, who was one of tens of thousands on the NYPD). A minuscule percentage of any population has that level of personal integrity and courage (maybe something like 1 in 40,000). Therefore, to influence a police culture toward unconditional respect, structural systems will have to be aligned with integrity-based social momentum and effective functional systems. (Examine Figures 2.1 along with 2.2a–2.2e, and their captions for one example of the rule of 30 at work. Then examine Figures 2.2f – 2.2h for another example.) Creating social support, structural support and functional support "sprouts" dormant anima and exposes those with vapid character (Now examine Figure 2.2i and 2.2j). As you have seen (Figure 2.1) The "Rule of 30" is built upon the "environmental structural" understanding of an organization. For now, Figure 2.1 illustrates the priority of the "anima environment" as foundational to all else. This figure will be explained and utilized in more detail in Chapter 9.

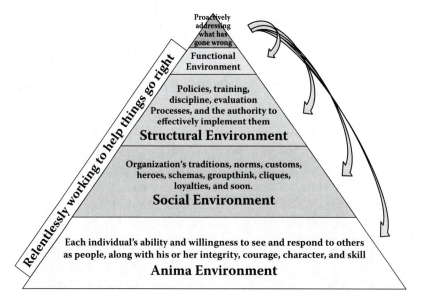

Figure 2.1

An individual will "act for what is right" when the total of all four
categories equals at least 30.

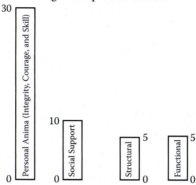

There are four areas that influence whether a particular individual will act for what is
right in any given situation: (1) the individual's personal anima, which includes not only
integrity and courage, but also the skill set necessary to effectively act for what is right;
(2) social support; (3) structural support; and (4) functional support.

(a)

An individual will "act for what is right" when the total of all four
categories equals at least 30.

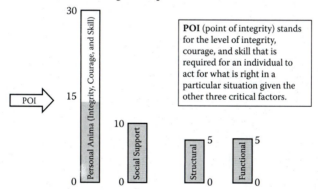

POI (point of integrity) stands
for the level of integrity,
courage, and skill that is
required for an individual to
act for what is right in a
particular situation given the
other three critical factors.

For example, an organization has strong policy, training, and systems of accountability around
clearing for service to answer calls and lower response time (a theoretical 5 on structural support).
At first, there is strong social support for this as well (a theoretical 10 on social support).
So when 5 + 10 = 15, someone with a personal anima score of 15 will act for what is right.

(b)

Figure 2.2

An individual will "act for what is right" when the total of all four
categories equals at least 30.

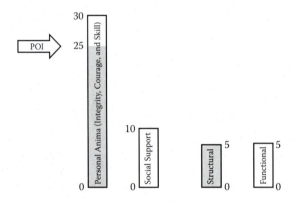

(c)

However, if proper equipment to do the task does not exist, officers (over 90% of budget cost in most
police organizations) at a patrol station find themselves waiting in line to use one computer terminal (less
than 1% of the budget). The lack of functional support (improper or insufficient equipment) begins to erode
social support down to zero (officers and sergeants as a group become frustrated, angry, and cynical).
So when 5 + 10 = 15, it now requires someone with a personal anima score of 25 will act for what is right.

An individual will "act for what is right" when the total of all four
categories equals at least 30.

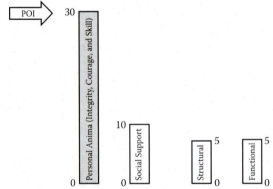

Over a short period of time, the structural support (policy, training, and accountability) becomes meaningless
at best and adversarial at worst. When policy is not supported both socially and functionally by decision
makers, the message is "This is not really important to our organization–it is simply a means to blame you
(end user) for what we (management) do not want to be accountable for."
**So when 0 + 0 = 0, it now requires someone with a 30 of personal anima to *even care* about what is right.
The primary issue at this point is, do they have the *skill* set to have respectful, relevant, effective
communications addressing the elephant in the room (the lack of functional support and eroded
social support)?**

(d)

Figure 2.2 (Continued)

An individual will "act for what is right" when the total of all four categories equals at least 30.

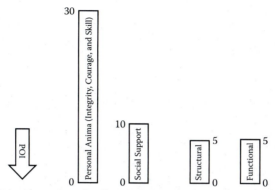

As bleak a picture as the previous illustration presents, it can be worse yet. In an organizational environment plagued by cynicism and apathy, *true accountability is unattainable* because there exists no touchstone to distinguish between those with high integrity and those with no integrity. High-integrity individuals are resisted, maligned, marginalized, and vilified in such a culture. This is because they keep having conversations no one wants to have and writing memorandums no one wants to read. In such an environment, problematic individuals are only identified when it is too late to do anything but take reactionary damage control steps.

(e)

An individual will "act for what is right" when the total of all four categories equals at least 30.

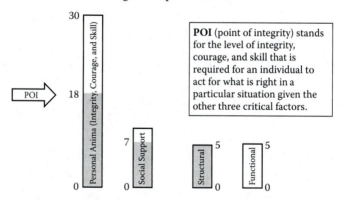

POI (point of integrity) stands for the level of integrity, courage, and skill that is required for an individual to act for what is right in a particular situation given the other three critical factors.

For another example, an organization rolls out a strong policy, training, and system of accountability based upon seeing all people as people and treating them with unconditional respect. It is early in the process so no one knows if this will be supported socially. However, the rhetoric and structural support from the top down that social support starts off with a 7.

So when 5 + 7 = 12, someone with a 18 of personal anima will act for what is right.

(f)

Figure 2.2 (Continued)

An individual will "act for what is right" when the total of all four
categories equals at least 30.

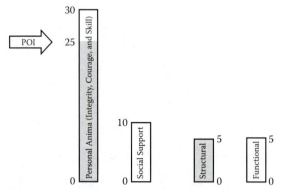

However, as soon as anyone is perceived as being seen as an object and treated in a disrespectful manner by management, social support drops to zero–UNLESS the manager is held responsible for the action.

So when 5 + 0 = 5, it now requires someone with a 25 of personal anima to act for what is right (see and treat members of our organization and community as people with unconditional respect).

This is an odd commodity–often, management is seemingly blind to what everyone else sees as clearly objectified treatment of members (see Figure 1.1 "String of Perils"). For example:

• Suddenly transferring a person (outside of normal rotations) without previous clear, respectful conversation.
• Transferring a tenured member to first watch (unless it is requested by the member) with no previous, respectful conversation.

(g)

An individual will "act for what is right" when the total of all four
categories equals at least 30.

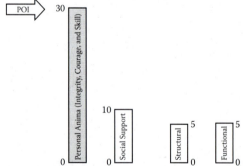

Over a short period of time, the structural support (policy, training, and accountability *around unconditional respect*) becomes meaningless at best and *adversarial at worst*. When policy is not supported socially by decision makers, the message is "this is not really important to out organization–it is simply a means to blame you (end user) for what we (management) do not want to be accountable for.

So 0 + 0 = 0, it now requires someone with a 30 of personal anima to *even care* about what is right. The primary issue at this point is, does anyone have the *skill* set to have respectful, relevant, effective communications addressing the elephant in the room (the lack of social support and eroded anima support)?

(h)

Figure 2.2 (Continued)

An individual will "act for what is right" when the total of all four categories equals at least 30.

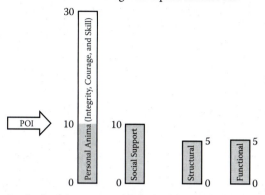

On the other hand, in an environment that has (1) STRUCTURAL SUPPORT (clearly written policies that are seamlessly linked to basic mission, high core values, and operational realities–and supported by correctly administered effective training processes), (2) SOCIAL SUPPORT (everyone from top to bottom actively supports and is accountable to the policy as stated), and (3) FUNCTIONAL SUPPORT (to the best of the collective understanding and ability), tools and recourses are properly allocated to allow the policies to be safely and efficiently carried out. *The minimum POI is only 10.*

(i)

An individual will "act for what is right" when the total of all four categories equals at least 30.

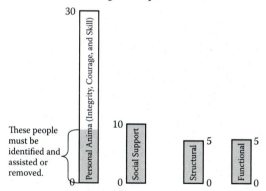

In an organization with full environmental support, those with very low integrity will stick out like a sore thumb. This will happen on minor issues without having to wait and react to the inevitable train wrecks of moral or systems failure. People with low integrity (9 or below) should be quickly identified, assisted, and/or removed, regardless of rank or loyalties. If this is not done, social support begins to erode and structural support becomes meaningless or adversarial.

(j)

Figure 2.2 (Continued)

As previously stated, the process of influencing the police culture toward unconditional respect will be dealt with in the last chapter (on *animating a culture*). For now, though, the bigger question instinctively burning in the hearts and minds of most law enforcement members is "Won't unconditional respect toward these 'assholes' compromise officer safety?"

Unconditional Respect
The Tactical Edge of Officer Safety

3

> To take offense at slight provocation is ridiculed as short-tempered and seen as weakness. True patience means bearing the unbearable.
>
> **—Bushido: The Way of the Warrior***

"Respect is not something you demand—it is something to be earned." I suppose I can't disagree with the first half of this statement. You can't expect people to respond to you with respect just because you demand it of them. On the other hand, true respect is "earned" by virtue of our individual existence. In a very real sense, respect can be considered the realization of another's intrinsic value as a human being and the accompanying degree of unpredictability—and thus danger—that comes with being human; therefore, it is possible to respect someone without requiring any particular behavior on his part. It is a fundamental truth; one can *choose* to have regard for another, while still recognizing the presence of differing value systems and memory schemas that render the other person potentially unpredictable. Respecting people is not a form of appeasement and does not require one to tolerate injustice or fail to take a stand for what is morally and ethically correct. The way you opt to conduct yourself when dealing with someone—especially someone who is difficult, rude, or even cruel—is a reflection of your character and personal commitment to a durable anima. It has little, if anything, to do with what she merits socially. It has to do with what all humans merit intrinsically.

As discussed in the opening chapters, anima is a very personal and private thing. Someone's anima represents not the image he projects to others, but what he actually is on the inside, deep below the surface. Anima deals not with outward actions (behaviors), but represents something much deeper and more meaningful. It is the true map by which we navigate the world around us, and it predicts our destiny. The modern-day servants of society need a consistent anima to serve as a type of "inner armor." This armor is worn closest to the heart and protects the noble servant from the insidious self-deception that seeks to undermine his ability to see the world consistently and correct the wrongs in himself and others.

---

* Inazo Nitobe, Bushido, The Soul of Japan (New York: G. P. Putnam's Sons, 1905).

In my current assignment, I lead a high-risk entry team, more commonly referred to as a SWAT team. The main purpose of our unit is to serve search warrants on suspected drug houses where evidence suggests there is a heightened sense of jeopardy (weapons, past violence, etc.). Recently, my team executed a warrant involving an armed felon who had a prior history of violence, which included the use of a firearm. The approach and execution of the warrant were practically flawless. The suspect—along with three others—was detained without a fight. We discovered he had prior felony convictions and was in possession of a loaded semiautomatic pistol and a substantial amount of crack cocaine. We moved the suspects outside onto the front porch because there was no electricity in the house and it was very difficult to see what we were doing. As my team began to search the residence for further criminal evidence, I observed a middle-aged woman walking down the road toward the house. She immediately began screaming profanities in the direction of my team. Her yelling brought other members of the neighborhood out into the street, and all of their attention was focused on us. I walked out to meet the lady. I introduced myself and asked her if I could be of assistance. She began screaming a stream of profanities at me, questioning my right to be on her property and to have her son in handcuffs. The more she became irrational, the more people seemed to gather around. I could sense she was rapidly gaining the support of the crowd, which was steadily growing.

A very typical law enforcement response to a situation like this would be to arrest the lady for disorderly conduct (which we actually define as "acting in a disorderly manner and causing a crowd to gather…"). Instead, I chose to listen to her. I didn't just listen to her; I listened to her with the intent to understand the true nature of her message. When she finished her verbal lashing of me, I stated, "Let me see if I understand you. You work two jobs to make ends meet. You don't get paid that much at work, so you can't afford to fix your car. You have to ride the bus to and from your jobs, which puts you at the mercy of the bus schedule. It also means you have to stand outside and wait for long periods of time, regardless of the weather. You worked hard today. You came home with the thought you would get off your feet and relax, but instead you find the police at your house and your son under arrest for selling drugs, and it upsets you very much." The lady responded by letting out a deep sigh, lowering her voice, and stating, "Yes, that does upset me." Our conversation took a very civil turn. I asked her some clarifying questions and could literally see the anger draining out of her face. The crowd that had gathered behind her began shrinking. The people who were initially attracted to the potential conflict became disinterested in a civil conversation. Once she felt like I understood her perspective, I launched into my detailed explanation of what brought my team to her home. I showed her a copy of the search warrant, which I explained to her in detail. I retrieved a jacket from her home and let her put it on so she could stay warm. The lady stood by quietly while my team spent over an hour collecting evidence and processing arrests.

How did my viewing this woman as a human with needs and fears, and my subsequent treatment of her at the scene of this warrant, reflect positively on our overall police mission? From an interpersonal communications standpoint, respect demonstrated my regard for her, her home, and our community, even in a very challenging circumstance. My inner way toward her, unconditional respect flowing from it, and subsequent treatment of her was in line with my agency's philosophy of building partnerships with our community.

These results were possible because my internal anima permitted me to be confident enough to listen to her message without being emotionally swamped by the content. It is interesting that "tough" officers regard emotions as weakness—except the emotions of anger and disdain toward others. "Tough" officers often wear anger and disdain as a badge of honor and always find ample reason (like this screaming lady) to justify their disdain. The sad irony is that anger and disdain toward others are the emotions most indicative of a weak personal anima. These particular emotions also render their "tough" holder tactically and interpersonally compromised.

What about the tactical perspective? I spoke with an officer recently who said he believed that being respectful gave officers the appearance of weakness and exposed them to serious officer safety concerns. He equated "respect" with softness. I suppose being "hard" would have meant arresting the lady for disorderly conduct, thereby sending a clear message to the entire neighborhood that no one can "disrespect" the police. I have traveled that road, and I can tell you what some of the results might have been:

- The middle-aged lady with no criminal record is placed under arrest for a misdemeanor charge—not a good use of a SWAT team.
- Because she is very emotional and feels justified in her anger, she doesn't go peacefully, and we have to use force to compel her compliance.
- The crowd, who is feeding off her anger, reacts to the arrest, and we have to make several more arrests. Since she resisted arrest, you better believe the others won't go quietly.
- When we use force, we don't pull punches, so it is almost a certainty one or more of the arrests will require medical treatment, along with at least one officer waiting at the hospital.
- My team—who are specially equipped to deal with violent felons—is taken off the street for a couple of hours filing misdemeanor charges that will likely tie them up in municipal court for months to come. The resulting convictions will most likely end with probation sentences and small fines.
- Word of the melee quickly spreads through the neighborhood, and a general attitude of distrust is either cultivated or reinforced. The

original purpose of my team being in the neighborhood—to make it safer and drug-free—is lost in the shuffle.

- There are ensuing community complaints and internal affairs investigations, which require a large time commitment to investigate. None of the complaints are upheld against the officers because we didn't "technically" do anything wrong. This fact serves to widen the gap between the police and the community, furthering distrust.
- The officers who must answer calls in that neighborhood are at increased risk and are viewed negatively by members of the community.
- The gun-packing, drug-peddling felon in the house becomes an instant folk hero in the neighborhood because he "stood against the roughshod police."

This type of action may have been consistent with the letter of what some consider "law enforcement," but does it honor the spirit of our basic police mission?

Respect is not a soft skill. Respect is a very "hard" skill that takes time and patience to develop. When I share this concept with fellow officers, a few of them are very receptive and open. Of those who aren't, the majority of the pushback comes from their idea that treating a suspect with respect will cause the suspect to view the officer as weak. This will in turn make the officer seem like a more attractive target for a physical attack. The attitude seems to be that if an officer "appears" tough and capable, then a suspect will question his own ability to successfully assault the officer.

This type of thinking is convoluted on many levels. First off, being able to "appear" tough and capable is no match for actually *being* tough and capable. Many officers claim that officer safety is of paramount importance. When I survey these same officers, they cite firearms proficiency and physical conditioning as very important in ensuring their safety on the street. When pressed further, most admit they spend little time working on either.

Second, there is often a stark contrast between what people say is important to them, and what actually is important to them. It is easy to claim that officer safety is a very serious concern, but it takes a great deal of effort to maintain the skills and attributes necessary to be a truly safe officer. There is no essential skill in law enforcement that is "easy" to develop, and that includes the personal confidence to display unconditional respect for others. Many officers who claim being respectful is dangerous are really just looking for evidence to justify the fact that they daily violate their own sense of right and wrong by treating people poorly. Justifications also allow one to blow off time at the range or skip workouts to make up the couple of hours of sleep one missed because of mindless activities like watching television. It may make an officer "feel" safer to posture and be verbally harsh to a suspect or a citizen, but this feeling is merely a by-product of a deep and dangerous self-deception. Unfortunately, a truly capable opponent can see right through posturing and recognize an easy target.

I think one fundamental reason behind the inclination to embrace the "Dirty Harry" mentality is that it provides an illusion of safety and security, which becomes one more justification for treating others poorly. Respect is often equated not only with softness but also with vulnerability. Most officers deal with feelings of vulnerability by one of two means—disengagement, or overcompensation in the form of directing anger and disdain toward others. Because the former (disengagement) is unacceptable in the police culture, the latter (anger and contempt) becomes the social norm. It makes us "feel" tough and capable if we "talk" tough and capable. In order to carry on that way on a daily basis, it is very necessary to objectify the people we come in contact with. By *objectify*,* I simply mean to see them, and treat them, as objects as opposed to what they obviously are—people. One other subconscious purpose of the objectification is that it makes others seem less like us, which would imply they are less capable of doing physical harm than we are. Remember, many police officers want to find a way to "feel" safe, without actually putting the time and effort into training that will allow them to "be" safe.

I offer this consideration to officers who feel they can intimidate subjects by excessive posturing and harsh treatment. Most of law enforcement's most dangerous clientele grew up in an environment of rampant cruelty and mistreatment. Some were abused physically and mentally on a routine basis and lived in constant fear of their surroundings. Many have been through the prison system and are much more experienced at fighting than the average police officer. The fact is that the police—who have "rules of engagement" to consider—are about the last group of people who would ever intimidate a hardened, dangerous criminal by berating them. In fact, it is considered common knowledge in law enforcement that candid interviews with offenders who have assaulted the police reveal that one of the few things that actually intimidate them is an officer who has a calm, assertive presence and looks like he "can handle himself." These criminals realize that the hallmark of a disciplined opponent is self-control. The irony in the "talk tough, appear tough" mentality is that the people it might actually intimidate are the people who lack the inclination to assault the police in the first place. However, almost anyone can eventually be instigated to fight-or-flight reactions through disdainful mistreatment. Both fighting and chasing are dangerous activities to officers, but chasing and subduing

---

* "**reduce to object:** to reduce somebody, or something that is complex and multifaceted, to the status of a simple object." From Encarta® World English Dictionary (North American Edition) © & (P) 2009 Microsoft Corporation. All rights reserved. Developed for Microsoft by Bloomsbury Publishing. http://encarta.msn.com/dictionary_/objectify.html (accessed September 19, 2009).

those who are disinclined to commit (and untrained in) violence becomes like a self-deluding drug. These little victories with unworthy, untrained opponents serve to delude officers into thinking that anger and disdain toward others serve them well and comprise a tactically sound alternative to personal character and commitment.

Lastly, demonstrating unconditional respect for others requires a strong sense of self-confidence in one's ability to use force when necessary. In fact, an officer who is not confident in his ability to deal with physical conflict will find it exceedingly difficult to employ an attitude of unconditional respect. In contrast, a truly strong and powerful person loses nothing by employing respect when interacting with even the most challenging of opponents. This theme is not exclusive to law enforcement.

On December 8, 1941, the 25th Army of the Japanese military launched amphibious and aerial attacks on Malaya, Singapore, and Hong Kong, which were then British Crown Colonies. Following the Japanese aggression, the War Cabinet of the British government authorized the declaration of war on Japan. Anthony Eden, England's foreign minister, was traveling to Moscow at the time of the attacks, so the oversight of the Foreign Office fell to Prime Minister Winston Churchill. The letter he penned to the Japanese ambassador read,

> *Sir,*
> On the evening of December 7th His Majesty's Government in the United Kingdom learned that Japanese forces without previous warning either in the form of a declaration of war or of an ultimatum with a conditional declaration of war had attempted a landing on the coast of Malaya and bombed Singapore and Hong Kong.
>
> In view of these wanton acts of unprovoked aggression committed in flagrant violation of International Law and particularly of Article I of the Third Hague Convention relative to the opening of hostilities, to which both Japan and the United Kingdom are parties, His Majesty's Ambassador at Tokyo has been instructed to inform the Imperial Japanese Government in the name of His Majesty's Government in the United Kingdom that a state of war exists between our two countries.
>
> I have the honour to be, with high consideration,
> Sir,
> Your obedient servant,
> Winston S. Churchill

Of the letter, Churchill later wrote, "Some people did not like this ceremonial style.
But after all, when you have to kill a man, it costs nothing to be polite."*

---

* Winston S. Churchill, The Grand Alliance, vol. 3 of The Second World War (London, 1950).

What Respect Is NOT

We must be careful not to confuse respect with friendship, admiration, or trust, all of which result from cultivating a personal relationship with another (trust is earned only by consistent, courageous conduct over a period of time).* The way we choose to treat others—especially when we have options—has little to do with them, but is instead a reflection of a personal commitment to our anima. To subscribe to the notion that someone else can extrinsically control our internal attitude by behaving—or failing to behave—in a particular way is a mechanism to absolve us of our personal responsibility for our conduct. What follows is self-deception, and although it may be a convenient way of justifying our behavior, it doesn't fool our conscious, which is the most suitable barometer for measuring the rightness of our actions. "When we need to be justified, anything that will give us justification will immediately take on exaggerated importance in our lives. Self-betrayal corrupts everything—even the value we place on things."†

Let us consider an example of just how corrupting self-betrayal can be. A couple of years ago, I was conducting a tactical briefing prior to serving a high-risk search warrant. I had requested a couple of officers from outside my team to come and assist us with perimeter security issues. Their job was to ensure no suspects escaped from the rear of the residence while my team was working to breach the fortified front door. Just prior to beginning the briefing, I happen to notice one of the officers who had arrived to help us was not wearing body armor under his uniform shirt. I was faced with a choice. My initial impulse was to pull him to the side and instruct him on the imperatives of wearing a vest while performing his duties. I instead chose to ignore the problem. I actually carried on with the briefing and disciplined myself not to look at the officer. In my mind, by not acknowledging there was a problem, the problem ceased to exist. Once I betrayed my sense of what I should do to help keep this officer safe, I began to see the situation in ways that "justified" my self-betrayal. I began to rationalize (i.e., tell myself rational lies about) my decision not to act for what was right:

- After all, the officer didn't work directly for me. I was not "his" supervisor. Therefore, he was not my responsibility.
- There were probably quite a few officers who didn't wear their vests. I couldn't possibly correct them all.
- His supervisor saw him everyday. Surely she knew he didn't wear his vest. If she didn't have a problem with it, why should I cause a stir?

---

* Gus Lee, Courage: The Backbone of Leadership (San Francisco: Jossey-Bass, 2006), 154.
† Arbinger Institute, The Anatomy of Peace (Salt Lake City, Utah: Arbinger Institute, 2006, 2008).

- I could see it plainly: if I corrected this officer, he would tell all his buddies that I was a hard-nosed "company" man. Why should my reputation suffer because he wasn't conscientious about his safety?
- This officer went to the same academy I did. He had the same training. Information is relative. He had obviously weighed the dangers and determined he was willing to risk not wearing a vest. After all, it is his life.

Taking these justifications into consideration, I was perfectly deceived into thinking that my failure to act to ensure the safety of this officer was not only the right choice but also the only logical choice. The truly insidious thing about this situation is that I wasn't the only person in the room who knew this officer was risking his life and the life of the others on the mission. Self-deception is contagious.

I finished the briefing and made my way to the tactical van to don my entry gear. While I was checking my equipment, one of my officers, Andy Keil, pulled me aside. He told me he had noticed the officer without a vest at the briefing, and he wasn't comfortable with the situation. Andy told me someone needed to address this issue. He said he thought it would mean more coming from me since I was a supervisor, but if I wasn't going to say anything, he would go talk to the officer himself. Andy gave me a gut check that shook me out of my apathy. His demonstration of courage empowered me to act for what was right, regardless of what others might think of me. Andy had shone a light on my cowardice and exposed my self-betrayal. After speaking with Andy, I pulled the officer aside and told him he could not go on the raid until he was properly equipped. I explained to him the dangers involved in the task and contacted his supervisor and asked her to procure him a new vest prior to allowing him to work in the field again.

Andy taught me a powerful lesson that day. It was as if I had attended Courage 101 right there in the parking lot. I was forced to examine my paradigms and realize I had failed to *respect* that officer. I did not value him as a person. I was more concerned about other people's perception of me than I was about his life. What I considered to be respectful—not risking an embarrassing exchange that could offend the officer—was actually *indulgence*, which is a deceptive and dangerous counterfeit of respect. Andy might not use these words, but he possessed a strong unconditional respect for his fellow officer.

The Tactical Side of Unconditional Respect

It is self-evident that unconditional respect for other members of society is a good policy from an interpersonal relations standpoint. However, a common kneejerk reaction in law enforcement assumes unconditional respect lowers one's tactical acumen. It "feels good" and instills a sense of bravado to think of these people as "assholes," but what if fostering certain attitudes in our unconscious mind forces us to miss subtle clues that could alert us to a suspect's violent intentions? Self-betrayal could prove lethal if it causes us to assign an erroneous value to the words or actions of someone who poses a legitimate threat.

As humans, we are incapable of observing anything without interpreting it based on our preexisting schemas. This reality is at play in all our interactions, even the most deadly ones. Consider Dr. Marc Green's research in the area of human factors as it relates to officer-involved shootings:

> Perception is the processing of applying stored knowledge to the sensory input and forming an interpretation. Once the image is sensed, the officer must decide whether it represents a gun or some other object based on what he knows and what he has learned through experience. When the sensory information is uncertain or ambiguous, as with low visibility, the cognitive factors grow in importance. This is a problem-solving task that humans address by using innate cognitive strategies. In psychology they are called "heuristics," general rules of thumb, or "biases." The term "bias" is not meant in the negative sense of everyday language. In cognitive psychology, a "bias" is a reasoning strategy that aids in quickly arriving at a correct answer. In critical situations, it is dangerous to engage in the slow process of conscious reasoning. Instead, the human mind has evolved heuristics and biases to speed the interpretation and to make sense of a complex situation.[*]

In other words, when we look at the world, we are actually looking in a mirror. What we see is more of a reflection of how we are than how the world actually is. Also worthy of consideration is the part our unconscious mind plays in affecting our perceptions of the world around us. Most of the processes that shape the decisions we make occur beneath our conscious awareness and are influenced by internal factors rather than external stimuli. Lieutenant Jim Glennon, a noted Street Survival Seminar instructor, notes,

> While it is the conscious mind that houses our subjectivity, morality, judgment, our ability to be self-aware and make rational decisions, it is our unconscious that is actually the controlling force in both dealing with our existence and in navigating our way through life.[†]

Glennon goes on to explain the unconscious mind is not simply feeling—it's actually thinking. The thought process is very rapid, and the results of the rapid thought process manifest as feelings. People are constantly communicating, and our subconscious minds are constantly interpreting that communication. This is never more important than in a tactical environment.

---

[*] http://www.visualexpert.com/Resources/policeshooting.html.
[†] http://www.policeone.com/patrol-issues/articles/1660205-Pre-attack-indicators-Conscious-recognition-of-telegraphed-cues/.

One of the most valuable tools a police officer possesses is the ability to engage in rapid cognition. This ability permits officers to make split-second, life-altering decisions under the most extreme of circumstances. Author Malcolm Gladwell explains that we use a method he calls "thin slicing." *Thin slicing*, or *rapid cognition*, refers to the ability of our unconscious to find patterns in situations and behavior based on very narrow slices of experience. This form of "snap judgment" is an *unconscious* process.*

As previously noted from Dr. Green, the way we see and interpret our world is significantly predetermined. It stands to reason that the image of people we hold in our minds is projected onto the people we interact with during the course of our duties. While firearms proficiency and reasonable use of force training are important to ensure officer safety, revisiting and refining our internal paradigms are critically important to keeping us safe. When we build internal schemas that justify a demeaning view of others, we leave ourselves personally and tactically compromised.

So, what are the tactical implications of our internal view of the world and the people we serve? Nearly all police officers agree that situational awareness is extremely important to officer survival, but the irony is that we often objectify others (i.e., see them as objects, not people), which in turn undermines our ability to cultivate a sound state of tactical awareness. Our very inclination to see people as objects "blinds" us and causes us to lose our situational awareness. We see others in ways that justify our preexisting view of them. The only way we can do this is subconsciously to disregard any data that does not support our preexisting view.† This amounts to self-induced myopia at best, and total self-deception at worse. This helps us to either devalue them or inflate their virtue, rather than achieving balance by recognizing their humanity. In that moment—unbeknownst to us—we have shed our anima, which amounts to taking off the warrior's inner armor. The implications of respect go way beyond making people "feel" good, and actually help to foster a personal regard that could save our lives.

Precontact Threat Assessment

Experience has proven that the subjective perceptions that an officer experiences during moments of peak stress can dramatically influence the tactics she uses when confronted with an immediate threat, especially when the time to respond is limited. If the men and women of law enforcement have

---

* Malcolm Gladwell, Blink: The Power of Thinking without Thinking (Boston: Back Bay Books, 2005).
† Richards J. Heuer, Psychology of Intelligence Analysis (Washington, D.C.: Center for the Study of Intelligence, Central Intelligence Agency, 1999), 9.

learned one valuable lesson from our fallen brothers and sisters, it is that no call for service or investigatory stop can be deemed "routine."

Police Officer Joshua Miktarian was no rookie cop. He was a decorated K9 officer with 11 years of experience who had worked the midnight shift for the Twinsburg, Ohio, Police Department since 1997. On Sunday, July 13, 2008, at 2:00 a.m., he initiated a "routine" traffic stop to investigate a driver for suspicion of playing loud music and driving while intoxicated. Two minutes into the stop, Officer Miktarian radioed for help. At the same time, a 911 caller reported hearing loud popping sounds and shouting at the scene of the traffic stop. Responding officers found Miktarian alone and suffering from multiple gunshot wounds to the head. Police tracked down the driver, Ashford Thompson, at his sister's home in Bedford Heights. When they arrested him at 2:41 a.m., he had one handcuff dangling from his wrist and was attempting to remove it by applying Vaseline to his arm. Thompson's shirt was covered in blood, and police found the murder weapon, a 9 mm pistol, in the residence. The Cuyahoga County coroner pronounced Officer Miktarian dead at 2:48 a.m. at Metro Medical Health Center. He was the first officer killed in the line of duty in the department's fifty-six-year history.*

Officer Miktarian's encounter with his murderer was the result of a traffic stop for a minor offense. This type of enforcement activity occurs thousands of times a day across the country and is typically concluded safely. Unfortunately, even the most seasoned officers cannot predict the nature of the people they will come in contact with on a daily basis. Ashford Thompson justified the murder of a brave public servant by declaring it an act of self-defense. Officer Miktarian was shot four times. Three of those shots were fired into his head as he lay helpless on the ground. If Ashford Thompson's claim of self-defense does not demonstrate the power and danger of internal justifications and the resulting self-deception, I don't know what would. But these internal justifications and self-deceptions are not unique to suspects; they are part of being *human*. That is why the development of a durable anima is so critical to officers.

Officers must prepare themselves physically and mentally in anticipation of these potentially life-altering or -ending events to ensure their survival and the survival of the people they are sworn to defend. Officers have no mechanism to determine the will and intent of a subject during the precontact phase of an investigatory stop. The safest mind-set for an officer to possess is one that helps assuage our blinding prejudices and preconceived assumptions based on experience in similar contexts. This safe mind-set is an anima that sees all people as people, is rooted in personal integrity, and is buttressed by courage, which manifests itself as unconditional respect for all.

* http://blog.cleveland.com/plaindealer/2008/07/twinsburg_officer_killed_durin.html.

This leads to the question "Can the manner in which an officer perceives a subject's innate value prior to a field contact be an asset or a liability?" It would seem the logical answer is "yes." When an officer disregards or offers feigned respect to a subject, he is essentially failing to value the adversarial worth of that particular person on an unconscious level. Certainly, we think, a "scumbag" is no match for a well-trained officer. The subconscious message is that a scumbag (or white trash, homeless drunk, crack head,* etc.) would lack the mettle to even initiate, let alone follow through with, a serious attack on the officer. We have disdain for people who threaten our value systems with their behavior, and that disdain blinds us to their unpredictability (humanity).

Police officers achieve social distancing by relegating the subject of an encounter to a subordinate level of the food chain. This quite typically and naturally allows the officer to lower her caution flag and drastically—sometimes fatally—underestimate the danger posed by the subject with whom she cannot identify.

> If you know the enemy and know yourself, you need not fear the result of a hundred battles. If you know yourself but not your enemy, for every victory gained you will also suffer a defeat. If you know neither the enemy nor yourself, you will succumb in every battle.[†]

> **—Sun Tzu**

What undesired effects can this tendency have on the filter through which the officer processes threatening behavioral cues? Consider the tragic case of New Orleans Police Officer Nicola Cotton. Officer Cotton, a twenty-four-year-old rookie police officer, stopped to investigate a suspicious man who matched the description of a rape suspect in the New Orleans Central City district. Police Superintendent Warren Riley later said Officer Cotton did not perceive the homeless suspect, Bernel Johnson, as a threat when she approached him in a crowded shopping area. She even radioed the dispatcher to relay that she did not need backup. The ensuing fight, which was captured on surveillance cameras, told a different story. When Officer Cotton tried to handcuff Johnson, a man twice her size, he pushed her away violently. When Officer Cotton gestured for Johnson to come closer, he attacked her viciously. Johnson was able to take Officer Cotton's baton and severely beat her with it. He then disarmed her and shot her fifteen times as she lay helpless on the street. Johnson held the empty firearm and waited for responding officers as Officer Cotton lay dying. Officer Cotton was eight

---

[*] Crack head is a derogatory term used to identify a person addicted to crack cocaine—source unknown.
[†] Sun Tzu, The Art of War, ed. Thomas Cleary (Boston: Little, Brown, 1988).

weeks pregnant at the time of her murder. Johnson was later determined to be a paranoid schizophrenic with prior arrests for vagrancy and disturbing the peace.*

During Contact: Awareness of Subtle Precursors of Violence

Utilizing our personal value judgment system to categorize someone as dangerous or harmless based on their perceived social value may make us feel comfortable, but it doesn't keep us safe. This mind-set predisposes us to failure and is exacerbated once we are face-to-face with a subject in an enforcement context. Labeling allows us to trick our minds into thinking we have the situation figured out. This self-deception is like a security blanket we wrap around ourselves to shelter us from our sense of vulnerability. It is comforting to "know" someone's capabilities because it helps mitigate the uncertainty of the encounter. The true deception lies in the fact that we have actually *increased* our tactical vulnerability.

Gavin De Becker, author of *The Gift of Fear*, writes, "The great enemy of perception, and thus of accurate prediction, is judgment. People often learn just enough about something to judge it as belonging in this or that category.... Familiarity is comfortable, but such judgments drop the curtain, effectively preventing the observer from seeing the rest of the play."† We do not fear what we think we understand, and we have an innate drive to categorize people.

Unfortunately, labeling suspects short-circuits the ability we have to perceive danger. Strategic awareness requires having regard for a person's humanity. In order to regard someone, we must first assign a value to him as a person—an equal. Once someone is viewed as deserving of less consideration based on his station in life, it follows that we devalue him in our unconscious mind. Conversely, when we think of him as humanly equal to us, we have more respect for the potential level of threat he poses.

Our perception of threat is influenced by two factors: attention and organization. Our preexisting schemas influence what information we attend to, and they channel our inferences and understanding of the information. We pay attention or select to attend to schema-consistent information. It is practically impossible to be appropriately influenced by information that is inconsistent with our schema for the individual we are dealing with. Instead of processing information about the individual,

---

* Colley Charpenter, "N.O. Cop Killed with Own Gun," *New Orleans Metro Real-Time News*, http://www.nola.com/news/index.ssf/2008/01/no_cop_killed_with_own_gun.html.
† Gavin De Becker, The Gift of Fear (New York: Random House, 1997).

we process information about the category we place them in and assume that it is accurate.* Jack and I sometimes refer to this as "virtual reality decision making."

The implications of this information on officer safety are vast. The way we choose (which may be an overstatement, because we are generally unaware of making a choice) to see others is the impetus for every observation that follows. In a very real sense, our personal levels of awareness and safety during an encounter are predetermined by our anima.

It has been said that we bring something of ourselves into every observation we make. It is for this reason that a truly "objective" observation is impossible. In each encounter, our brains must filter literally thousands of pieces of information and assign a value to each one. Most observations occur at a subconscious level, so this process of value assignment helps determine which observations are forwarded to our consciousness and awarded further scrutiny. This type of "selective perception" is more about our expectations than about reality. Paradoxically, the selected observations are delivered in the form of emotions that often eliminate our ability to intelligently scrutinize. "We are constantly bombarded with so much sensory information that it is impossible for us to pay attention to everything. Our subconscious mind scans our environment and selects what it deems important for us to notice."† Even then, we tend to see what we expect to see.

Consider the case of former Grand Rapids Police Officer Matthew Dwyer. Officer Dwyer's performance evaluations indicated he possessed above-average judgment; however, he lost his job after using what was deemed poor judgment during a disturbance call where a fellow officer lost his life on July 8, 2007. Officers from the Grand Rapids Police Department responded to investigate a domestic disturbance at the home of Jeffery VanVels. VanVels hid inside the garage with a loaded shotgun and ambushed Officer Robert Kozminski, shooting him in the head as he approached up the driveway. Fellow officers were able to take VanVels into custody immediately after the shooting. Other officers were attempting to rescue the mortally wounded Kozminski, when Officer Dwyer—who was covering the house from another position—believed he saw VanVels moving inside the house and fired a shot at what he believed to be the suspect. The shot created confusion among the officers tending to Officer Kozminski and interfered with their rescue efforts. Dwyer still maintains he saw someone in VanVels's home that day. But authorities have said the family's dog was the only thing inside when the officer took his shot. The police department investigation into Dwyer's

---

* J. M. Darley and P. H. Gross, "A Hypothesis-Confirming Bias in Labeling Effects," Journal of Personality and Social Psychology 44, no. 1 (1983): 20–33.
† Steve W. Williams, Making Better Business Decisions (Thousand Oaks, Calif.: Sage, 2002).

actions determined not only that he didn't see VanVels but also that his shot caused stress for other officers on the scene and interfered with the "rescue of Officer Kozminski."*

There is plenty of research on the subjectivity of perception that supports Officer Dwyer's belief that he observed the suspect in the house—even though he simply wasn't there. Attention, particularly under high stress, has a single, undifferentiated, limited capacity and reduces our ability to process information. This is termed *selective attention*. Perceptual narrowing that occurs under these conditions results in more information being processed about that which we are attending to (selective attention), but it significantly restricts or blinds us to information that we are not paying attention to. This is called *attentional blindness*.[†]

We have already discussed the fact that, as humans, we are incapable of looking at anything without interpreting it. This is a natural condition. Let us revisit the notion of how we perceive an object differently than a person. When we look at an object—like a glass or a bowling ball—our brains process the information we receive through filters that regulate perception before it is brought into our conscious awareness. Much the same process occurs when we look at a person; however, the portions of our brains that light up when we process human beings work in dramatically different ways and at a different speed. When we look at people, we employ a part of the brain called the fusiform gyrus to process information during the interaction. It is a very sophisticated, fast-working mechanism that acts much like a supercomputer. In contrast, when looking at an object, we utilize a completely different and less powerful part of the brain—the inferior temporal gyrus. If the fusiform gyrus is like a supercomputer, then the temporal gyrus can be compared to a pocket calculator. It is much more simplistic, methodical, and slow moving.[‡]

Studies support that as little as 7 percent of communication between humans is content. The other 93 percent is made up of a combination of emotional messages through voice inflection, facial expressions, and physical movements.[§] The 7 percent represents "what" is being said, and the 93 percent is the "how." Let's consider the implications of this information. When we see others as less than we are, we see them not as human beings, but as objects. When we objectify them, we employ the part of our brain that processes objects, and this part of our brain is not as suited for picking up on the emotional content of communication. How important is this information

---

* http://blog.mlive.com/grpress/2008/03/report_grand_rapids_officers_a.html.
† William Lewinsky, The Attention Study: A Study on the Presence of Selective Attention in Firearms Officers, Force Science Institute. http://www.forcescience.org/articles/attentionstudy.pdf.
‡ Gladwell, Blink.
§ M. L. Knapp and Anita L. Vangelisti, Interpersonal Communication and Human Relationships, 3rd ed. (Boston: Allyn & Bacon, 1996).

considering that the most dangerous encounters a police officer experiences are drenched in emotion?

While humans seem to have an innate intuitive ability to sense danger, most people are more inclined to employ denial than to actively engage in developing such a life-saving attribute. Denial is an option, but not a very desirable one for someone who places himself in harm's way on a daily basis and relies on his perception as a survival mechanism.

Police officers are often called upon to use force during the performance of their duties. Some subjects of law enforcement scrutiny have little compunction regarding the initiation of both non-deadly and deadly attacks on law enforcement officers. As previously mentioned, there are often many preassault indicators that are presented by the offender but not immediately recognized by the officer who becomes the subject of an assault. Developing the ability to recognize a threat as it is unfolding and to act automatically in the moment to counteract it, is an essential officer survival skill. The foundation for this ability arises from training and experience with similar stimuli. Unlike an animal, which can be trained using simple conditioning techniques, a human being has the ability to circumvent cognitive training by making a conscious—or unconscious—decision to devalue the information or threat. Anima, therefore, becomes the source of our attitude; and attitude is much more important than natural aptitude or skill development when learning survival techniques. The ability of an officer to integrate these survival skills depends largely on her anima—which determines one's personal philosophy.

An officer who adopts an internal anima of integrity and courage manifested as unconditional respect will be more likely to be naturally observant, not subconsciously blocked, to the subtleties of an encounter than an officer who allows his personal values and biases to cloud his objectivity. Unconditional respect can be understood as treatment of an individual that is not predicated on any particular behavior on her part, but is instead a product of the officer's anima, which is rooted in integrity and courage. An officer who operationalizes the philosophy of unconditional respect will be better able to detect subtle changes in a subject's behavior that could be precursory to an assault.

An officer can actually be able to sharpen his objectivity by disciplining himself to internally view all subjects in a consistent manner, thereby creating a sharper focus on reality, as opposed to looking at a situation with the limitations inherent in a preconceived bias. This train of thought belies the concept that the highly touted option of exhibiting "feigned" respect is sufficient, and instead encourages officers to focus their efforts on character-building exercises and self-evaluation. As we will discuss further in Chapter 6, even if an officer is an expert at "faking it," she cannot conceal her true feelings from others. Her behavior will undoubtedly be influenced by these internal factors, regardless of what attitude she outwardly displays. In essence, the age-old adage "We reap what we sow" has never had a more critical meaning.

Use of Force: Closing the Hesitation Gap

Fostering an internal anima of unconditional respect for the people we encounter is ultimately in furtherance of the mission of law enforcement. We must attempt to remove the dictated social value judgments that cloud our vision of the situation in order to make correct decisions without hesitation. An officer must rely on an intentionally developed anima to overcome the tendency to make demeaning judgments and take action driven by the resulting emotions. Fear is an example of an "emotional" reaction, and we work hard to manage it because we see some of its effects as self-limiting. In reality, all of our emotions are nothing more than subjective impressions of the world around us, and the value of any given emotion is completely dependent on the anima or value system that it is predicated upon. Emotions stemming from an anima lacking in integrity are misinformed at best and dangerous at worst.

Almost anyone would acknowledge that treating people with unconditional respect would result in a lower incidence of public dissatisfaction and community complaints, but, as we have discussed, it will help us make proper, defensible decisions and even keep us safe.

Consider for a moment the quality of "righteousness." The best way to describe this concept is with analogy. Let's assume you have a very strong opinion regarding the *immorality* of abortion, an issue in our culture that is surrounded by heated emotions. You are enrolled in a debate class, and your teacher instructs you to prepare a position paper in *defense* of abortion. Now, from an academic standpoint, there is no doubt you could put together facts and inferences that would pass muster and meet the requirements of the assignment, but how convicted would you be in that position? I think it would be much more challenging than preparing a paper that opposed abortion, which in this example is a position you strongly support.

There is a certain quality—call it *righteousness*—that envelopes a person's actions when he pursues goals that are consistent with strongly held values. There is a higher quality of effectiveness that is present when strong conviction meets purpose of will.

A comprehensive study on law enforcement officers killed in the line of duty demonstrated that 85 percent of officers who were slain during the performance of their duty never discharged their weapons in defense of their own lives.* A comprehensive review of 148 incidents of law enforcement officers being killed from 1998 through 2000 indicated that 125 (84.5 percent) of the victim officers never fired a round at their killer.† Most citizens do

---

* Federal Bureau of Investigation, 1992 FBI Uniform Crime Report (Washington, D.C.: Federal Bureau of Investigation, 1992).
† U.S. Department of Justice, FBI Law Enforcement Officers Killed and Assaulted (Washington, D.C.: Federal Bureau of Investigation, 2000).

not appreciate that many officers, given circumstances where they could use deadly force, refrain and hesitate until the last possible moment or do not use it at all. If police officers shot 50 percent of those who assaulted them with weapons, they would shoot approximately 5,000 people annually. The reality is that police shoot and kill about 350 individuals each year, a number that dramatically illustrates the frequency with which officers refrain from using deadly force.*

In other words, while the pervasiveness of excessive force complaints should be a concern to law enforcement, we also need to honor the reality that the large majority of officers are typically inclined to hesitate during crisis and use *less* force than is needed to overcome a threat, even at the very real risk of losing their lives. A strong personal anima can help resolve both the use of excessive force and the tendency on the part of officers to hesitate and expose themselves (and as a result, others) to unnecessary risk when faced with physical threats that require immediate action.

I served as a firearms and defensive tactics instructor with the Kansas City, Missouri, Regional Police Academy from 1999 to 2003. One of my duties was to review all use of force incidents involving members of our department. I once reviewed an in-car video of one such incident involving a young officer. The officer was confronting a combative male subject. The officer reached out and struck the subject on the leg with his baton. What struck me as odd was the fact that the officer's strike appeared to be extremely half-hearted and ineffectual. The subject apparently didn't think much of it either, because he became even angrier and the fight escalated rapidly. The subject was eventually subdued with the aid of assisting officers. I conducted a follow-up interview with the officer who had struck the subject with his baton. I asked him why he had struck the subject with such little force. His reply was very honest and spontaneous. He stated, "I wasn't sure if I *should* hit him, so I just thought I would kind of hit him."

The implications of that statement are astounding. When officers use force, it should be the high point of righteousness of action and should be professionally carried out with as much skill and vehemence as the officer can generate. An officer should be completely confident in the correctness of his actions and put the full measure of his skill into the righteous use of force. Anything less could prove, and has proved, deadly.

We need to work from the ground up to ensure we do everything within our power to address the obvious—and, perhaps, not-so-obvious—reasons for this phenomenon. I propose that if an officer has the strength of character to demonstrate unconditional respect for an adversary, then she will be

---

* Shannon Bohrer, Harry A. Kern, and Edward F. Davis, "The Deadly Dilemma: Shoot or Don't Shoot?" FBI Law Enforcement Bulletin, March 2008, http://www.fbi.gov/publications/leb/2008/march2008/march2008leb.htm#page7.

empowered to use whatever force that is objectively reasonable to control that person during an attack, not only physically but also psychologically. When the officer knows, on a very deep, subconscious level, that her actions are not predicated by judgmental, socially charged prejudices, but are driven by objective criteria, she will possess just the sort of righteousness I am proposing. As a result, she will be able and willing to give the full measure of effort in pursuit of high-valued goals.

One way of understanding respect is to think of it as a balanced concept. There are essentially two ways to demonstrate "disrespect" for someone you come in contact with. The first way, which we have previously discussed, is to devalue them. An unintended consequence of that decision is that we devalue their ability to harm us. Disrespect also comes into action when we inflate the virtue of someone with whom we have not developed a trusting relationship. This occurs when we make snap judgments based on personal biases and experience. We have already established that we have a tendency to feel more comfortable distancing ourselves from people who we perceive as not sharing the same values. It also follows that we feel more naturally trusting of people we see as being similar to us or sharing the same ideals. Many agencies have experienced the loss of officers due to their inability to properly categorize someone as potentially dangerous during an encounter. The result is that when the person becomes suddenly violent, the combination of the officer's ensuing hesitation and the rapidly evolving circumstances creates an extremely deadly situation.

Anima: An "Internal" Code

The pursuit of a highly developed anima will allow police officers to adhere to principles rather than capitulate to the natural proclivity to devalue others, and thus become self-deceived. Codes of conduct rooted in values are not new concepts, and have in fact been employed in many cultures to guide the protectors of societies in the performance of their respective duties. Most of these codes are of an "external" nature and deal with the outward behaviors of the individuals or groups. They are powerful guiding forces in the cultures of warriors and peacekeepers who are charged with defending the people. Dr. Shannon E. French notes,

> In many cases, codes of honor seem to hold the warrior to a higher ethical standard than that required for an ordinary citizen within the general population of the society the warrior serves. The code is not imposed from the outside. The warriors themselves police strict adherence to these standards[,] with violators being shamed, ostracized, or even killed by their peers. One

historical example comes from the Roman legions, where if a man fell asleep while he was supposed to be on watch in time of war he could expect to be stoned to death by the members of his own cohort. The code of the warrior not only defines how he should interact with his own warrior comrades, but also how he should treat other members of his society, his enemies, and the people he conquers. The code restrains the warrior. It sets boundaries on his behavior. It distinguishes honorable acts from shameful acts. Under the codes of chivalry, a medieval knight had to offer mercy to any knight who yielded to him in battle. In feudal Japan, samurai were not permitted to approach their opponents using stealth, but rather were required to declare themselves openly before engaging [in] combat. Muslim warriors engaged in offensive jihad could not employ certain weapons unless and until their enemies use[d] them first.*

The exercise of self-discipline is no less important for the protectors of modern society, but it is especially relevant to the police because of the unique relationship we have with the public that does not allow us to exist as a separate entity. The "codes" that regulate behaviors have undergone monumental change and adaptation as societies matured; however, the principles that govern the men and women who accept the task of serving society are timeless.

The men and women who make up the modernized police forces of the world are in desperate need of a code or "inner way" that will protect them not only from the criminal element but also from the perils of their own tendency to deceive themselves. The type of code we are advocating is not an external one, but begins inside the individual officer. It does not simply address behaviors, but instead deals with something much deeper than behavior. It deals with our inner way, which actually *determines* how we interpret the world around us. This code—or anima—is meant to be used as a "character map" to help those granted with extraordinary responsibility to focus their talents in the pursuit of a life of honorable service.

This brings us to the important point of drawing a distinction between the job of a soldier and the duties of a police officer. Many comparisons have been made to police officers and soldiers, and while most are harmless attempts to identify with long-standing traditions rooted in honor, some of the best of us have lost touch with the basic mission of law enforcement. The military culture and the police culture share some similarities, such as proficiency with weapons, initiation rituals, and service to humankind; however, their basic missions differ drastically. The purpose of a soldier is to defend his cultural ideals from outside forces that work to destroy or conquer a society. A police officer works within the social order to protect it from self-destruction. A soldier fights an invading enemy, while a police officer builds

---

* Shannon E. French, The Code of the Warrior: Exploring Warrior Values Past & Present (Lanham, Md.: Rowman and Littlefield, 2005).

partnerships with others in society to encourage compliance with laws. This is necessarily the only way to ensure the operation of a "free" society. A soldier kills to overcome enemy forces, while a police officer uses deadly force only in impartial service to the Law to maintain social order.

The police are more often viewed—and actually view themselves—as an occupying force that responds to the neighborhood when there is trouble and withdraws once they have restored the status quo. Where it was once the job of the culture and social norms to keep people's behavior in check, we are now dependent upon the government to handle even the most minor of infractions. In this social milieu, the police and the citizens they are sworn to partner with in instilling safety and prosperity come to view their mutual interactions with an "us versus them" mentality. It has become fashionable for officers to adopt an adversarial perspective toward the public, especially when they perceive the public as being unsupportive or overly critical of their actions. This distorted perception reinforces the idea that the police are a separate entity from the public and can result in a pattern of self-justification that can be used to legitimize rudeness, a lack of empathy, and, in some cases, illegal behavior. This kind of unconscious programming—reaffirmed over hundreds of interactions and years of typecasting—is the inevitable result of a police culture that has slowly drifted away from a service mentality. Having the ability to change the oil in your car does not make you a mechanic. Having the ability to use force effectively—as a soldier or a police officer—does not make one a warrior. A warrior understands that the most important battle to be fought is an internal one. It is the battle against our own tendency to be self-deceived about ourselves and others that demands the warrior's attention above all else. The key to understanding others—even our enemies—resides within us, and that knowledge and pursuit of the anima that will facilitate it are what define a warrior.

As public administration authors Kim Ward and Ernest Crist note, "The 'us versus them' mentality manifests itself in two ways: an adversarial relationship with administrators and alienation from the public. Workplace cultures that are riddled with non supervisory employees, who display an 'us versus them' mentality toward administrators, do not occur by accident. Specific behaviors prompted and nurtured its development."* It seems like a logical conclusion that feelings of alienation that are allowed to manifest within a police agency will eventually be expressed outwardly as a lack of respect and empathy for members of our community with whom we have a social contract.

---

* Kim M. Ward and Ernest L. Crist, Strategic Planning: A Leadership Tool in Preventing Corruption, Misconduct to Corruption, Avoiding the Impending Crisis, June (Washington, D.C.: U.S. Department of Justice, Federal Bureau of Investigation, 1998), 18–20.

This type of "class distinction" serves to widen the gap between the police and the communities they patrol. Officers feel more comfortable distancing themselves from subjects mentally, physically, and emotionally, which permits them to dehumanize the most challenging of their clientele, but inevitably dehumanizes everyone geographically or racially associated. This makes it much easier to justify mistreatment on the part of the officer, and makes indecision inevitable because the decision-making centers of our brains are overloaded with inaccurate, overly subjective data. Although the citizenry have a natural fear of crime and disorder, it becomes more tolerable if such apprehension must compete with the fear of mistreatment by the police.

As mentioned in the introduction, modern leadership treatises focusing on personality ethics while eschewing the foundational principles of character development have insidiously worked their way into the fabric of popular culture. The law enforcement community has bought into the idea that we somehow stand apart from the rest of society and "police" the citizens. The truth is that our officers not only are members of the communities we serve but also should exemplify the best qualities of humanness. This is not to say that police officers should not be capable of performing tasks well above the capabilities of the average person. There must be a balanced approach to develop an extreme sense of accountability and honed skills. This will empower heroism and prevent the protectors of society from becoming disgusted with those people who cannot, or choose not to, protect themselves. This kind of antipathy toward the average citizenry lays the foundation for abuse of power and mocks the foundational principles on which our country was founded.

We must work to develop a high degree of anima to be able to model high core values regardless of the context in which we find ourselves. This type of anima, rooted in principle-based values, serves as a breastplate to protect the heart of the righteous servants of our culture, not only from the physical threats they face on the streets but also from the more threatening internal tendencies that work to instill complacency and erode character. This provides a base for unconditional respect and the tactical edge of officer safety.

I Hear Every Word You Say, but I Can't Listen Should I Care?

4

Unless a person is hearing impaired, hearing simply happens—sound is perceived. Listening is different: you must consciously choose in order to process meaning from words. "Most people tend to be 'hard of listening' rather than "hard of hearing."*

Could it ever be possible that listening, understanding, being influenced and appropriately responding to the content of someone's message, be a matter of life and death, or career survival for an officer?

The Kansas City, Missouri, Police Department (KCPD) Board of Police Commissioners fired two officer is an unusual case. In February of 2006, Officers Schnell and Spencer stopped Sofia Salva for displaying a fake temporary tag on her vehicle. She

> …repeatedly told the officers she was pregnant, bleeding and needing to go to the hospital. The officers wouldn't take her though, and they didn't call an ambulance. They arrested her on outstanding warrants…. Salva, who was almost four months pregnant, miscarried the next morning after spending the night in jail.[†]

This scene is tragic on many levels. Recent news reports now indicate that even immediate medical care could not have saved this pregnancy. However, early in the investigation this possibility hung like a dark cloud over Ms. Salva and the officers. In the aftermath, the KCPD lost two trained officers and was the subject of national embarrassment and litigation. And two officers, whose previous experience and character could otherwise speak for them, lost their careers and were paraded before the nation as representing much of what is wrong in law enforcement.

What follows is a thought process that is not the result of any "insider" information about the tragedy summarized above; we have no more information than does any member of the public. This is simply an outsider's perspective about possible root cause factors underlying this disturbing event, an

---

* University of Minnesota, Duluth, "Hearing versus Listening," 2006, http://www.d.umn. edu/kmc/student/loon/acad/strat/ss_hearing.html (accessed August 18, 2008).
† KMBC.com, "Board: Cops to Be Fired in Miscarriage Case: Pregnant Woman Requests Treatment during Traffic Stop," posted and updated May 23, 2008, http://www.kmbc. com/news/16377833/detail.html (accessed September 6, 2009).

attempt to consider at least two important factors that potentially bear upon the issue. First are organizational social structures and training processes that are stated and intended along with social contracts that are unstated and unintended. Second, consideration will be given to the effects of individual memories that potentially cloud judgment and social interactions. After these considerations, I will propose a possible answer to the looming question: "Why do intelligent officers with no significant history of disciplinary action calmly and intentionally do what turns out to be a career-ending act in front of their in-car video camera?"* The following analysis could very well miss the mark, but no one will ever know until police departments that have access to the complete investigative files begin to do comprehensive root cause analysis investigations. These types of investigations have been common in the military, in aviation, and in medicine for decades. At the time of the writing of this chapter, the KCPD is at the beginning stages. The KCPD is learning to ask the tough questions, such as the one posed above and to seek out the answers. Under Chief James D. Corwin's initiative, "Blueprint for the Future," the Management and Decision Making Committee spun off a subcommittee, the Judgment Interference Factor Initiative (J.I.F.I.) Committee, of which I (Jack) am the designer and chair. The committee consists of law enforcement members with varied backgrounds, and civilians who have critical roles related to law enforcement. We are bringing in consultants such as an ethicist; a risk management expert; a scientist in human cognitive, visual, and attention limitations; and airlines trainers in human factor awareness. The goal is to build a comprehensive program from the ground up. Ultimately, we hope to learn to proactively identify and mitigate the factors that link the tasks of law enforcement to accidents and calamities. See the final chapter of this book, "*Anima*ting a Culture," for more discussion of the initiative. For now, after a discussion that is intended to explain how personal memories and organizational social and training processes can possibly impede listening, possible mitigation tactics will be examined.

Memories That Can Impede Listening

There seems to be a quiet revolution slowly spreading into the conscience of professionals worldwide. The science seems crystal-clear and compelling but, at the same time, so counterintuitive that it is effortless to ignore the implications of it. The world is being challenged to rethink basic presuppositions about how the human brain perceives and records events. Consider this brief

---

* "Officers Fired over Use of Taser Gun: Police Board Says No Back Pay, Benefits for 2 Officers," http://www.thekansascitychannel.com/news/4754689/detail.html (accessed September 4, 2009).

overview statement regarding memory by the British Psychological Society Research Board.

Memories are records of people's experiences of events and are not a record of the events themselves. In this respect, they are unlike other recording media such as videos or audio recordings, to which they should not be compared.* (Emphasis in original)

The board goes on to explain that single events alone do not form memories, past experiences become part of current memories. Therefore, even a memory that contains specific detail does not insure that the event actually happened as remembered. People can in fact remember events they did not even experience: "these are often referred to as 'confabulations.'"

With the use of DNA testing, there has been a wave of people released from prison who were convicted of crimes by what was once considered preeminent evidence: eyewitness testimony. Much to the chagrin of those tasked with prosecuting criminals, it seems that the human brain is designed more for personal survival (recalling and reacting to danger) than reliable eyewitness testimony.

What follows is an attempt to explain these findings about memory from one layperson to another, to demonstrate a possible connection between the findings and the question posed above: "Why do intelligent officers with no significant history of disciplinary action calmly and intentionally do what turns out to be a career-ending act in front of their in-car video camera?"

The human mind operates by building a series of schemas that contain images, ideas, words, and, most importantly for survival, emotive content. So, for example, a small child who has never been burned by a wood-burning stove may find the stove a warm and intriguing thing just waiting to be touched and explored. The parents must be diligent to protect the child from his curiosity and ignorance because the child has no preexisting schema from which to be wary of the stove. However, once the child has been burned by the wood stove, a parent may find that the same child who was once drawn to the stove is now no longer comfortable to even be in the same room with it. Now when the child sees the stove, rather than feeling interest and curiosity, he feels fear and repulsion. Based on the new schema—the memory of having been burned—the child now has an autonomic response that delivers emotions of fear animated by adrenaline, cortisol, and other stress hormones. It is important to note that the stimulus, the sight of the stove, has not

* British Psychological Society Research Board, Guidelines on Memory and the Law: Recommendations from the Scientific Study of Human Memory (Leicester, UK: Research Board, 2008).

changed; only the schema for interpreting the stimulus has changed. It is also important to note that because the stress response happens many times faster than the cognitive processes of the brain (i.e., conscious thought), it is almost impossible to simply "decide" to not have the stress response.

The following is an event that illustrates how this phenomenon can work with an adult in a position of authority. As a father of five children, I (Jack) have visited the state facility where one goes to be tested for a driver's license more than once. On one such occasion, my sixteen-year-old son had driven away from the building to take his driving test with the state examiner in the passenger seat. Upon his return, I was amazed to see him end the test by executing a flawless parallel-parking maneuver. I was even more amazed to find the examiner literally out of control with fury and rage upon exiting the vehicle. "Good luck with that one!" the examiner spat out through clenched teeth as she pointed back to the dumbfounded youth. It was quickly evident, based on the examiner's statements, that she likely has or had a very confrontational relationship with her own "rebellious and disrespectful" teenager. Apparently, my son had made a facial expression that clicked a subconscious, autonomic response in the mind of the examiner. As an autonomic response, all the emotive content related to *her* teen spewed out toward the youth who happened to be in front of her. I surmised this because she referenced her own teen early on and then, about halfway through her tirade, she looked back at my son, who was looking down and shaking his head in response to her verbal attack on his character. When she saw him shaking his head, her voice went up two octaves and she screamed, "There he goes again!" During this time, the examiner had been rendered physiologically incapable of (1) cognitive reasoning, like "As a professional, I have no business being this out of control, condescending, and rude to this man and his son"; and (2) actual listening. Because of the stress hormones coursing through her brain and body, she was geared up only for fight, flight, freeze, submit, or posture. In this case, she was in some combination of posturing and fighting with my son and me. I surmise that what was being played out looks much like how she likely does (or used to) fight and posture with her own teen. It was easy to see that if my son or I had an emotionally charged schema around the behavior of the examiner, a disturbance of significant proportions would have ensued. Based on her "hair-trigger" reaction to a common facial expression, it is natural to postulate the examiner has a toxic relationship with her teen. But, of course, she will always blame her teen for the toxicity of the relationship; after all, the *teen* is the disrespectful rebel (see a reference to the Arbinger principles of nonviolence at the end of this chapter). As it was, I simply listened to the examiner until she had vented her anger enough to become rational. I then took my son to get his license photo while explaining to the hapless youth what had just happened to him.

A Schema Built

Now take the issue from the view of a youth in the community. Imagine the appearance of a uniformed police officer at a typical middle school. The responses to such an occurrence can be as varied as the people who experience it. One youngster may have a response of fear and terror at the mere sight of a uniformed police officer; another may have a response of relief and joy. Others will have every emotion between these two, including indifference. The individual responses are almost exclusively a commentary on the preexisting schemas in the minds of the individual youths and have almost nothing to do with the individual officer. Consider a possible schema for the youth with the terror response. Let us suppose that several years earlier, as a spoiled two year old, he walked into a small corner café for lunch with his parents. Entering the café, he spots the gumball machine by the register. He expresses he wants a gumball but is told, "No." He is led away from the brightly colored gumball machine crying and eventually refuses to eat his lunch in protest of not getting a gumball. In a state of exasperation, his parents point out two uniformed officers seated nearby. They tell the toddler in a foreboding voice something that frequently makes officers around the country cringe: "You see those two officers over there? You better shape up; if you don't settle down, they will take you away to jail!" Now, this is the first time the little boy has ever paid any attention to uniformed officers, and his impressionable young mind does *not* reason, "Oh, my parents are using hyperbole, a figure of speech designed to manipulate me because they wish to avoid their parental training responsibilities." Rather, the young boy is terrified, and his mind creates a schema that has the image of uniformed officers along with all the terrible fear and emotions related to the concept of being ripped from his parents' arms and taken away because he wants a gumball. Eight years later, the now ten-year-old youth is in his home playing with his brother early one Saturday morning. Unbeknownst to them, the next-door neighbor has come home drunk from an all-night binge and assaulted his children. The police have been called, and the first two officers have also been assaulted by the enraged, drunken man. An "assist the officer" call has gone out, and the ten-year old looks outside after hearing the sirens arrive on his street. The youngster sees five officers dragging his "poor" neighbor out of his home in what seems like an overly aggressive manner using "harsh" holds and pain compliance techniques (most of which the man is immune to in his drunken rage). In an instant, the old schema is brought out (again, many times faster than cognitive processes), and the new, terrifying (although incomplete) data and emotion are added to the already disturbing memory. Three years later, the young man is at middle school, spots a uniformed officer, and has an immediate response (again, many times faster than cognitive processes) of terror and fear, based on the old schemas but precipitated by the current image.

A Schema Reacted To

Now look at this scenario from the officer's perspective. The officer came to do a fun life skills program with the youth of that middle school. When he detects the above-mentioned young man's "deer in the headlights" response, in a millisecond the officer experiences a subconscious release of stress hormones, physiologically preparing the officer for a fight, flight, freeze, submit, or posture event (regardless of the fact that policy and social construct leave the officer only the option to posture). Years of training, street experience, and locker room banter have given the officer a schema that interprets overly fearful, furtive, or hostile expressions as precursors of violent behavior or evidence that criminal activity is afoot. The officer is instantly filled with suspicion: "What's this _____ up to?" The youth had his own personal schema brought to the event, and the officer had a completely opposite schema of the same event and automatically reacted to the reaction of the youth. The only thing the two colliding schemas have in common is the uniform worn by the officer. Everything else is different and unrelated but *assumed* by both parties to be related.

Pretend that later, the officer was to listen (not likely during the initial stress response) to a trusted teacher. The confidant tells the officer that the student in question is not a criminal or even any kind of trouble maker; in fact, the young man is a model student both academically and socially. But the teacher has no idea what the student's schema about the police is, and because of the teacher's differing schema, she does not detect what the officer does. The officer would likely fall into a self-justifying, other-condemning loop of thinking that goes something like "Who does this kid think he is, being angry at me or afraid of me and hating me? He doesn't even know me; I came here to be friendly, and he's being a jerk."

Any time we deal with memory and the resulting experience, we must understand that we are dealing with a reconstruction of one's experience, not a recording. What the stimulus before us is has little to do with what gets recorded as the memory. The memory and emotions we have around an event are really a *biography about us* more than the event.

> People understand the world through "schemas" and "scripts," stereotyped mental models of objects and events. When they recognize a situation, either in perception or in memory, they invoke the most applicable schema or script and may unconsciously fill in missing information in order to complete the reconstruction.[*]

---

[*] Marc Green, "Eyewitness Memory Is Unreliable," Visual Expert Human Factors, http://www.visualexpert.com/Resources/eyewitnessmemory.html (accessed August 18, 2008).

These factors not only present an obvious problem for a prosecutor who is attempting to build a case upon human memory, but also can render effective interpersonal communication extremely difficult and counterintuitive. Why? Let us return to our student and officer in the middle school. The youth is terrified and fearful; the officer is suspicious and/or resentful; but neither one knows, nor cares, why the other has the perspective and emotions that he does. If they interact verbally, the emotions and attitudes they both bring to the event will be communicated (see Chapter 6) and will poison the interaction. The youth is already fearful and terrified (with good cause in his mind); as a result, all the officer's words and actions will be interpreted through that schema. Because the officer is already suspicious or resentful of the youth (with good cause, in his mind), all the youth's words and actions will be interpreted through that schema. In a best-case scenario, neither the youth nor the officer will likely be trusted, believed, or treated with dignity by the other, even though *this has nothing to do with who the individuals really are.*

It is the height of irony that the officer came to the school to engage in an example of what is known as *community policing*. But interpersonal issues running below the surface undermine and poison the efforts with unwarranted stress responses and hormone releases. In fact, in my limited experience, officers frequently and naturally find the community members who are most involved and active in community-policing efforts to be the most irritating people to deal with.

In a best-case scenario, *efforts to support the systematic use of partnerships get lost in the unchartered territory of interpersonal presuppositions and stress hormone bewilderment*; in a worst-case scenario, a dangerous circular process could possibly have been initiated. Early research on rat brains seems to indicate this possibility.

> [F]indings suggest that even when stress hormones spike for reasons not related to fighting, the side effect of lowering attack thresholds may still precipitate violent behavior.... Their stress hormones rise, facilitating the onset of aggression and making them more likely to become violent in seemingly benign settings.[*]

When Schemas Collide

What does this dangerous circular process look like when played out in everyday life? A typical "road rage" incident could be very instructive. On November 27, 1996, two young women squared off on Interstate 71 in

* Rachel Adelson, "Hormones, Stress and Aggression—a Vicious Cycle: Rat Research Shows a Feedback Loop between Stress Hormones and the Brain's Attack Center," APA Online, Monitor on Psychology. American Psychological Association, 2004, http://www.apa.org/monitor/nov04/hormones.html (accessed August 30, 2008).

Cincinnati, Ohio. One irritating provocation led to another and developed into a rage-driven brawl. The aggressive dual between these two young women continued to escalate to the point where a mother of two did a final aggressive maneuver and forced the other woman's car into a crash, severely injuring her and precipitating the loss of her preborn baby. The mother of two then went to work and bragged about her conquest, using profanity to express her satisfaction in the justness of her cause. In the end, not only was a preborn baby lost but also the mother of two was convicted of aggravated vehicular homicide and aggravated vehicular assault. She was sentenced to a one-and-a-half-year prison term.*

Obviously, if rage and aggression loops can begin with something as normal and benign as a daily commute or a Little League sports game (as is often seen), it is easy to see how the potential exists in police work. Currently, to mitigate this ever-present reality:

- Officers are repeatedly conditioned to have trained responses to aggressive or violent behavior, to replace natural reactions
- Officers receive stress inoculation or force-on-force training to lower the natural effects of hostility
- Officers receive training in tactical communications processes designed to promote compliance to verbal commands and assist officers in presenting a professional presence

Unfortunately, training sometimes has unintended results. These unintended results can remain undetected for years, even decades. We do not claim to have this "figured out"; we are simply advocating that questions be asked and answers be sought, rather than simply blindly accepting tragic results as unexplainable lapses in judgment, such as the example this chapter opened with.

Training That Produces Unintentional Results

Now consideration will be given to how a training process dating back to the 1970s produced unintended deadly results. The phenomenon will then be considered in light of the current discussion, "Why do intelligent officers with no significant history of disciplinary action calmly and intentionally do what turns out to be a career-ending act in front of their in-car video camera?"

* Leland R. Beaumont, "The Importance of Emotional Competency: Avoiding the Tragedies of Emotional Incompetence, 2005–2008, http://www.emotionalcompetency.com/need4.htm (accessed September 1, 2008).

What Can Be Learned from the Past?

Law enforcement trainers have learned to be aware of three domains during the training process:

> *Knowledge—to inform*: provide information or knowledge about a policy or procedure
>
> *Attitude—to persuade*: be an agent of change in order to help overcome objections to new ideas, procedures, processes, and responses
>
> *Skills—to train*: help personnel develop necessary skills so that they become fit, qualified, and proficient

So, for example, to effectively introduce and teach racial-profiling stop report processes, members may do the following:

- Receive instruction on legal and procedural issues surrounding racial profiling (knowledge)
- Be provided with reality-based explanations and examples as to how and why racial profiling is bad for law enforcement, our community, and officers' careers. Ideally, members would be given an opportunity to understand racial profiling from the perspective of someone, preferably in law enforcement and the community, who has been harmed by it (attitude)
- Members would view videotaped scenarios of stops, be provided with forms related to the reporting process to fill out, and then proofread each other's work (skills)

Leaders and trainers in law enforcement have learned by painful trial and error that *all* training is *always* affecting all three domains regardless of whether it is done intentionally or not. This learning is the result of the

> poor training methodology of the '70s[,] when we were busy policing our brass [picking up the portion of the cartridge that remains inside a revolver after the bullet is shot].... Cops were then found dead in gunfights with their brass policed.*

For example, consider the now infamous Newhall, California, incident in 1970:

> [F]our members of the California Highway Patrol ... were martyred at the hands of illiterate ex-convicts.... At least one of the officers was found

---

* Training Specialist and AZ POST Board Chairman Mark Zbojniewicz, Def. Tactics Subject Matter Expert Committee, quoted in Force Science News 64 (January 26, 2007): http://www.forcesciencenews.com/home/detail.html?serial=64.

clenching fired and spent .38 caliber casings in his cold, dead hand, the result of an instinctive reversion to range training during the firefight.*

At many police ranges even into the 1980s, when the revolver was empty officers were instructed to holster an empty weapon and then place brass in a bucket or stack them on a table in front of them before moving to the next stage of fire. This was to keep the range clean and safe. Everyone "knew" that during a *real* gunfight, the officers would reload and come back on target. What the trainers apparently failed to realize is the above principle: *all training is always affecting all three domains regardless of whether it is done intentionally or not.* In the stress of battle, officers were doing exactly as they had been *trained* in the psychomotor skills area, not as they had been *taught* in the cognitive domain.

The sad reality is that the ignorance and deadly wrong perspectives of the 1970s that led to the situations previously described by Zbojniewicz and Hankins (above)[†] were still ingrained in the training processes well into the 1980s. *It was as if reality was pounding on the intellectual door of law enforcement for over a decade, and few were hearing the knock.* It is our humble opinion that through the Salva case and others, reality is pounding once again. Does the profession stay on the old familiar road of firing the officers, constricting policies, and scratching its collective head? Or does it do the hard work of asking tough questions and examining long-held paradigms?

---

* Chris B. Hankins, "The New Paradigm: Police Trends toward More Powerful Handguns and the Mental Aspects of Combat Survival and Training," Criminal Justice Institute School of Law Enforcement Supervision session 24, November 8, 2004, http://www.cji.edu/papers/HankinsChris.pdf (accessed September 7, 2009). While the "picking up brass" account is widely accepted, Brian McKenna reports that the California Highway Patrol officially denies the "picking up spent brass" portion of the account. See Brian McKenna, Officer Down! Lessons from the Street (Calgary, AB: Warrior Spirit Books, 2008). On the other hand, my Leadership Academy partner Daniel Schmer has vivid memories as a boy growing up regarding the Newhall incident. Dan's father, Robert Schmer, was a lieutenant on the Missouri State Highway Patrol (MSHP) and the assistant director of the MSHP Training Academy in 1972. Dan recalls his father traveling to San Luis Obispo, California, where "Newhall CA Lessons Learned" training was conducted. Dan vividly remembers his father returning with a picture of empty brass lined up on the bumper of a patrol car reportedly found in front of where an officer had been slain. Lt. Schmer returned to Missouri a man burdened to change training processes at the MSHP Academy. The MSHP Academy had countertops that folded down In front of officers while in the range stalls. The counters were used, among other things, for officers to stack their brass during range-training cycles. Dan's father was later the director of the Academy and still later the administrative bureau commander over the Academy. In 1989 Dan's father succumbed to cancer while still in service to the MSHP. Dan explained that his sister also served on the MSHP and retired as a sergeant. Dan said she told him that when she went through the MSHP Academy in 1976, the counters were still there, but they were not allowed to utilize them, and specifically were told to avoid "stacking the brass."

† Zbojniewicz, quoted in Force Science News; and Hankins, "The New Paradigm."

Bringing Old Lessons Forward

Now, back to our question and the consideration of training processes that impede listening. Remember our principle, learned above: training (and internal social processes, for that matter) always affects all three domains (knowledge, attitude, skill) regardless of whether it is done intentionally or not. Many tactical communications processes, dating back decades ago but still in use to this day, teach a feigned or tactical respect. The idea is that officers can hold any internal attitude toward a citizen, as long as they assume a professional persona to meet the public. In Chapter 6, we will see that current research has solidly debunked the myth that one can hide an internal attitude of disgust from another person. For now, it has been explained how memories can create prejudicial internal attitudes of anger and disgust, which in turn render one almost incapable of listening and being influenced by the content of another person's message. *Does training that excuses these internal attitudes as inconsequential inadvertently foster such poisonous internal attitudes? Does this create a dangerous subconscious reality much like those of the officers who were distracted by spent brass during gun battles?* It would seem that the possibility of this is so significant to law enforcement that the question must not only be asked but also maybe even assumed to be true. After all, what possible benefit is there in not challenging internal attitudes that foster debased internal biases about other people?

Supporting Listening and Interpersonal Effectiveness

The final chapter of this book will present in some detail how to "animate" an organizational culture, but here is a quick summary relevant to the discussion in this chapter.

Focus on and Support Anima

Let us consider the data captured above regarding memories and schemas along with the Arbinger Institute's findings on the implications of internal attitudes toward others.* You will observe a dangerous, iterative cycle that directly plays into the issue at hand. The reasoning starts with the obvious point that all people are people. While the statement is simple and seemingly obvious, the implications are immense. Being a person means that they have brought past memories, schemas, fears, needs, hopes, and desires into the interaction that are unique to them. They (and I) will interpret this interaction through the

---

* Arbinger Institute, "The Arbinger Principles of Nonviolence," http://www.arbinger. com/downloads/principles_of_non_violence.pdf (accessed July 22, 2008).

grid of experience. Caught up in my own schemas, needs, and fears, I naturally ignore (act as if they are not relevant) their schemas, needs, fears, hopes, and so on.... By doing this, I ignore their humanity, which compromises my safety and reduces them to object (nonhuman) status. Once I see them as objects, that creates a state of extreme dissonance between us, and the stage is set for interpersonal problems, hostility, and violence. Because this is happening at preconscious and subconscious levels on the part of both parties, it creates a continuously deteriorating cycle that is self-perpetuating (feeds off the reactions of each other). The only way to interrupt this destructive process is to address the internal anima of at least one of the parties toward the other. Thus our flagship statement: the profession of law enforcement requires a personal anima that sees all people as people, and is rooted in integrity, buttressed by courage, and expressed as unconditional respect for all people.

Challenge Poisonous Social Norms

When subcultures use epithets to label people in other subcultures, it supposedly serves to instill esprit de corps and make it easier to "deal with" the social repugnance of the other subculture. It does neither. It actually creates cycles of conflict and distrust both between the subcultures and within each subculture. What it tells someone within the epithet-using subculture is "This is how I will treat you if you get outside the fold." What it creates between subcultures is the deteriorating cycle captured above. Further, research has repeatedly demonstrated that people are favorably predisposed to be violent or abusive toward others because of something as seemingly innocuous as a one-word dehumanizing label.

> [A] 1975 experiment by psychologist Albert Bandura, PhD ... found students
> were more apt to deliver what they believed were increased levels of electrical
> shock to the other students if they had heard them called "animals."*

Now back to consideration of the tragedy of the pregnant woman and the two officers. The best way to address this may be to pose rhetorical questions and answers that assume knowledge of the social, structural, and training issues raised in this chapter and the issue of personal anima of the previous chapters.

- What if training processes, organizational systems, and social structures consistently confronted condescending or dehumanizing attitudes toward any and all members of the organization and

---

* Melissa Dittman, "What Makes Good People Do Bad Things?" APA Online: Monitor on Psychology 35, no. 9 (October 2004): http://www.apa.org/monitor/oct04/goodbad.html.

community, and built accountability processes around negative biases rather than gave them tacit approval?

- Negative prejudicial presuppositions would be dragged out into the light and challenged against enduring principles of right and wrong. (See Figure 2.1a–2.1j.)

- What if unconditional respect for all people (versus the natural tendency toward conditional or earned respect) was the social and structural norm for an organization?

  - Every contact with members of the community would result in fostering promoters of the basic mission of law enforcement. This would build a natural foundation for community policing.

- What if all supervisors and commanders were accountable to always have an internal attitude of unconditional respect toward each other and all line element personnel as both social inspiration and a cultural norm setter?

  - This would produce zero tolerance for rude, condescending words or manipulative behaviors toward anyone.

- What if all members were encouraged to separate liking, trust, and reward from respect, and held accountable for this? In other words, even if you know someone is a criminal, a liar, and untrustworthy, you still unconditionally respect him.

  - This would enhance officers' ability to truly listen to and be influenced by the content of anyone's message, including nonverbal precursors to violence or aggression.

- What if internal organizational silos were dismantled and replaced with the social networks and systems structures that promoted safe, open, honest communication?

  - This would result in continual improvement, expanding trust, and excited stakeholders, thus unleashing the natural talents of members.

Conclusion

Unconditional respect provides the basis for effective training, social inspiration, and system processes within any organization. Unconditional respect enhances listening and communication—this increases officer safety, effortlessly builds community partnerships, and leads to effective problem solving. This is the *true* essence of community policing.

Anima-Based Leadership 5

We must become the change we want to see in the world.

—Mahatma Gandhi

Most of us are part of a culture that has conditioned us to look out for number one. Our entire society is structured to support the assertion that you have to be self-interested if you are going to "get ahead." There seems to be one thing that almost all people have in common: we want more. More money, more power, more control. We want to feel secure in the notion that we are the masters of our own destiny. We seek to control as many outcomes as possible. The irony is we are not in control. We are all subject to the timeless principles that govern the world. When we learn to align our behaviors with these principles, it is only then that we have some measure of control over our lives.

When we (the authors) share the philosophy contained in these pages, much of the pushback we receive from the supervisors and managers in law enforcement includes statements like "We have a paramilitary command structure and we need to be more authoritative like the military leaders. We don't have time to be compassionate or consider the feelings of those who report to us." I couldn't agree more with the first part of this statement. The large majority of police departments in our country (the KCPD included) are representative of a paramilitary organization. This is the most effective and practical model for law enforcement and has also served the men and women of the U.S. Army well since 1784. The U.S. Army's leadership manual—*Field Manual 22-100, Army Leadership*—makes the assertion, "Your people are human beings with hopes, fears, concerns, and dreams. When you understand that will and endurance come from emotional energy, you possess a powerful leadership tool."[*] This reflection stands in stark contrast to what most of the people I talk with think of when they imagine a "military" style of leadership. To the uninitiated, the military leadership model is characterized by the mindless enforcement of rules and the objectification of the individual soldier. The image that often comes to mind is one of a drill sergeant

---

[*] Army Leadership, Army Field Manual 22-100: Be, Know, Do, August (Washington, D.C.: Headquarters, Department of the Army, 1999).

61

screaming orders at a hapless private. The Army uses the acronym LDRSHIP as a guideline for its leaders:

- Loyalty
- Duty
- Respect
- Selfless service
- Honor
- Integrity
- Personal courage*

If we in law enforcement are encouraged to embrace a military-style philosophy when it comes to leadership, count me in. If this type of value system works well for the most powerful fighting force on the face of the planet, then I am confident it should be part of any law enforcement influence effort.

In the face of current challenges, if our society is going to continue to function and not collapse upon itself, the statement "To those to whom much is given, much is required" could never have more importance. The leaders of our society need a different paradigm. It is incumbent upon these leaders to build systems of accountability around an inner way that is rooted in integrity, buttressed by courage, and expressed as unconditional respect for all people. In order to possess this degree of unconditional respect, we must first recognize those whom we interact with as people with hopes, needs, dreams, and fears equal to our own. Some popular management theories unintentionally (and some intentionally) promote objectifying direct reports. These theories imply the numbers generated in statistical categories can measure performance and determine value. A subordinate who produces more is valued, and one who produces less is unworthy of personal regard. An anima-based culture, however, turns conventional wisdom upside down and challenges preconceived ideas of what it means to be the "boss." First assumption challenged: rank has its privileges (RHIP). To many, this phrase means that the higher the rank one attains, the more perks he is entitled to. Promotion means, among other things, a nicer car, a bigger office, and more money.

Consider how this notion contradicts the stated values of most police agencies. I have had the opportunity to teach supervisory personnel from law enforcement agencies all around the world. I always ask them what the stated values of their organizations are. One of the most common responses is "Our people are our most valuable asset." This sounds like a very inspiring concept. Anyone would want to work for an organization that values its employees in that manner. The problem is that stated values such as these rarely transfer

* Training the Force, Army Field Manual 7-0, October (Washington, D.C.: Headquarters, Department of the Army, 2002).

from the vision statement to the operational environment. Most of the organizations that claim to value their line personnel consistently reserve the closest parking spaces and biggest offices for the higher-ranking members. Consider this for a moment. The people who are the most valued (respected) members of the organization and accomplish the most concerning the basic mission have to walk the farthest to get in out of the weather.

An anima-based leader recognizes the concept of RHIP to be something entirely different. This type of leader understands that the privilege conferred on her is the *privilege to serve others*. The higher the rank one attains, the more people she gets the opportunity to support, encourage, and serve. Such leaders understand that they are accountable not only to the public, but also to the people whom they outrank—the people who put their trust in them. Consider the defining attributes of a leader related by the Greek Xeones, who testified to the death of the Spartan king Leonidas at the historical battle at the pass of Thermopylae:

> [A] *king does not command his men's loyalty through fear nor purchase it with gold; he earns their love.... That which comprises the harshest burden, a king lifts first and sets down last. A king does not require service of those he leads but provides it to them.*[*]

The mantle of leadership comes with much responsibility. People do not follow you for money or benefit packages, and they surely do not risk their lives for such things. They follow you when they believe in you and know you care about them and have their best interest in mind. A leader exists to serve his people, not the other way around. Once you as a leader accept this, you will unleash influential power you never imagined existed.

This chapter will discuss the place that anima-based leadership has in the new paradigm the authors are advocating for our profession. It is important to note that the type of leadership we will discuss is not limited to increase in rank. Rank only grants the bearer the positional authority to tell others what to do. Anyone can do that with a minimal amount of basic training and motivation. Anima-based leadership is rooted in the notion that the power to lead is actually conferred by the people who are led. It takes strict discipline to execute the duties of a leader in a manner that will inspire loyalty and trust. It is critical for the leader who bases her decisions on a strong inner way to place a high value on serving others.

A key component of anima-based leadership is the ability to exercise discipline to ensure the achievement of collective goals and objectives. Unless a leader possesses the ability to discipline herself, he will be ineffective at inspiring others to employ self-accountability. The most effective way to

---

* Steven Pressfield, Gates of Fire (New York: Bantam, 1998), 360.

influence others is to demonstrate the desired behavior on a consistent basis; it stands to reason that a leader must constantly strive to cultivate essential skills that are rooted in a solid anima. Once a leader has developed a foundation of character, he is able to focus on growing his competence—the second all-important piece of the puzzle—and an essential prerequisite for behavior modeling. That is not to say that one cannot work to develop both character and competence at the same time, but a strong character is foundational and helps ensure that each competency acquired is reconciled with high core values. Great skill alone does not make an effective leader, and each competency can be perverted and twisted without vetting it against the road map provided by a stalwart character.

Whether the issue is one of character or competence, it is all too tempting to try to master all of the desirable qualities and skills at once. This alluring approach is one of the pitfalls of supervisory models rooted in persona-based management frameworks. The problem is that when an aspiring leader—or anyone for that matter—attempts to focus her efforts on changing several aspects at once, the change effort becomes watered down. She essentially spreads herself too thin. The type of leadership we are advocating requires the insight to discern the areas where change will be most productive, and the personal discipline to direct attention to one critical element at a time. The remainder of this chapter will focus on the two critical components, character and competence, that every leader must grow in order to inspire others and create an environment where safe, honest, open communication results in better ideas and improved service to the public.

Character

Character is the essence of who we truly are, as opposed to the image we might portray to others to attempt to sway their perception of us. In a person of character, words and deeds are indistinguishable from one another. Rigorous pursuit of a powerful and effective anima is what develops character. When one seeks to:

- develop his inner way in accord with a sense of integrity and dedication to service of others
- grow his courage in the face of adversity over a period of time

the result is a mature character. This maturity aids in making challenging decisions about right and wrong. This type of character is obligatory for any person who desires to lead others and motivate them to stand on principle and act for what is right as opposed to what might be popular or expedient.

Before a leader can grow any of the competencies mentioned in this chapter, it is essential he makes a personal commitment to develop a solid foundation of high character on which to build them. Leaders are subject to much scrutiny and criticism. They hold a position of high visibility and as such are the perfect targets for denigration when a project or mission fails to meet its stated goals and objectives. It requires a sustained character to overcome the negativity, push onward in the face of ridicule, and humbly learn from our inevitable mistakes. Character forms the bedrock of a leader (as oppose to an efficient manager, who may function in some organizations with very little character), and it is upon that foundation that competence grows. Character naturally nurtures the skills and tools needed for a leader to defend his decisions and learn from his mistakes. Character development will be discussed at greater length in Chapter 8.

Competence

A strong character is essential for any leader of merit, but it is not enough when it comes to inspiring others to achieve more than is required of them. A leader must cultivate technical skill in her area of expertise to be able to build an ever-developing character, the pursuit of high core values, and a commitment to hone critical skills into the lives of people she seeks to influence. The people who would learn from you must have the sense that you can hold your own in the performance arena. A leader must be trusted in order to be capable of bringing out the best in others, and the people who follow her must have faith in her relevant knowledge, ability to execute around the organization's highest priorities, and decision-making ability. A leader must be able to get the job done.

Almost all of the skilled firearms instructors I know can shoot circles around the average shooter. They have mastered the fundamentals of firearms proficiency and developed their skill during countless hours of focused practice. They realize that their students will judge them on not only the merits of their character but also their ability to perform, which reflects on their personal level of credibility. While one hallmark of a successful leader is the ability to succeed through the efforts of others, there is no substitute for being able to demonstrate high skill in your chosen field. An aspiring leader should constantly improve his individual level of performance in all areas relevant to his role. The people a leader seeks to inspire need to see that following the leader's advice and example will have a payoff in the form of improved performance and effectiveness. This is a critical and often overlooked component of many influence strategies. Let us turn our attention to some vital core competencies in the area of anima-based leadership.

Humility

Humility makes great men twice honorable.

—**Benjamin Franklin**

It is incumbent upon all leaders to courageously challenge the wrongs within their organizations. The ability to do so is based upon the leader's level of personal commitment to right wrongs within herself. The development of this competency requires much patience and focused effort. Humility does not come natural for most, but it is essential for a leader. Being humble can be seen by many as a sign of weakness, but nothing can be further from the truth. A person who demonstrates true humility is one who has faith in her own abilities, and at the same time can subordinate her ego and desires to the mission at hand. A humble leader seeks to be productively self-critical and stays open to new ideas. Humility allows us to embrace change and share credit with others, thereby creating a climate that promotes the open exchange of ideas and encourages creativity.

Without a strong sense of humility, it is easy to think we have all the answers. After all, they promoted me to sergeant, captain, major, etc.; doesn't that mean I am supposed to be the best and brightest? While most recognize this logic to be patently foolish, those with positional authority all around the world subconsciously operationalize this philosophy daily. If we fail to cultivate a sense of humility, we become stubborn to a fault in defense of our ideas. Our ideas, which should simply be tools to help attain our objectives, become our identity. We are blinded to alternative perspectives by our closed-minded viewpoint that is rooted in our misperception of ourselves (self-deception).

Think of how failing to practice humility plagues us in our personal lives. We "compete" with family and loved ones to be right in matters small and large. We sometimes go to great lengths to prove another wrong in order to buttress our own sense of self-worth, all the while damaging the relationships we purport to value most. This competition occurs when we misinterpret matters of preference as matters of principle. What is truly more important: "winning" an argument over trivial things that will not matter an hour from now, or working to strengthen relationships by understanding and valuing differing perspectives? The answer is obvious; however, common sense is not typically very common.

The same dynamic is at work in the professional lives of leaders who do not foster open, honest discourse around their decisions. This self-centered approach stifles creativity and serves to "dumb down" the group. Humility improves the quality of relationships and encourages open-minded approaches to problem solving. The brightest among you may not be wearing the gold bars.

Leadership author and executive coach Bruna Martinuzzi has this to say about the competence of humility:

> We often confuse humility with timidity. Humility is … the antithesis of hubris.… It's about being content to let others discover the layers of our talents without having to boast about them. It's a lack of arrogance, not a lack of aggressiveness in the pursuit of achievement.*

The burning need some feel to bully others into adopting their viewpoint is rooted in a deep sense of insecurity and cowardice. A strong, principled-centered anima prevents the lack of self-confidence that stifles cooperation and creative effort around important goals. Humility is essential for the leader pursuing a strong inner way and provides the opportunity for personal and professional growth of himself and others.

Credibility

The more you are willing to accept responsibility for your actions, the more credibility you will have.

—**Brian Koslow**

An effective leader must be able to deliver on the promises she makes. Even the best-laid influence strategies will fail miserably if the leader lacks credibility. Consider a police sergeant at a community meeting who encourages community members to take a united stand against crime in their neighborhoods. She must also ensure the members of her team have the skill, expertise, and willingness to protect the community members against retaliation from the criminal element. If people do not have confidence in a leader's ability to make good on her promises, there is little chance the leader can effect lasting change.

When a leader's credibility is well established, the information she gives to the people she reports to permits them to make spontaneous, confident decisions, based on their faith in the quality of her character. To this end, having influence so that others consider an alternative viewpoint is essential for a leader. Well-established credibility helps to create an environment where others can be open to differing perspectives (refer back to the problem of blinding, preexisting schemas in Chapter 4). Some leaders assume that if their decisions are consistent with the basic mission of the organization and rooted in high core values, the people they report to will automatically be

---

* Bruna Martinuzzi, Mind Tools, 2006, http://www.mindtools.com/pages/article/newLDR_69.htm.

inclined to accept them on face value. The reality is that each of us brings our own unique viewpoint to every observation and evaluation we make. First a leader must be confident that a course of action aligns with high core values and the basic mission of the organization. Then, it is her responsibility to maintain a social environment that permits others to consider the merits of adopting the plan. The more credible she is, the more likely she will be able to influence others. The amount of credibility a leader possesses generally predicts the amount of trust others will extend to her.

The degree of credibility a leader will attain is directly proportionate to his willingness to accept responsibility. When I accept responsibility for a problem, I am open to the possibility of effectively responding to the problem. If I refuse to be "response-able," I have no possibility of responding. I essentially render myself ineffective at best and irrelevant at worst when I assign blame to external sources that are outside my sphere of control.

I (Chip) recently dealt with this issue with my youngest son, Brandon, who just turned sixteen and was anxious to buy a car. He applied for and got his first job working at a local restaurant. His job occasionally requires him to work late on school nights. Shortly after starting his job, he was late to school twice in one week. My wife, Krista, addressed the issue with him, reminding him it was his responsibility to balance his obligations. Brandon immediately blamed the fact that he was late on his alarm clock. He reported that he set the alarm each night, but it would occasionally fail to go off. Krista suggested that by blaming the problem on the alarm clock (an external factor), he was not only avoiding responsibility but also making it impossible to fix the underlying problem (he wasn't planning a proper amount of rest into his schedule). Brandon assured us the alarm clock was to blame. In an effort to build the relationship and give him an opportunity to learn, we went to the store and he purchased a new alarm clock. He bought new batteries and tested the new alarm several times. After he was satisfied that the alarm was in good working order, he went to work. He worked late that evening and did not get to bed until midnight. I happened to be in the kitchen when he came down the next morning—two hours late for school. He looked at me and said, "Dad, I know what you're going to say, but I have a really good excuse this time. I put the new alarm clock in bed with me so I would be sure to hear it. *Something* must have happened during the night because *it* shut off."

What Brandon failed to see eludes most of us when we shy away from accepting responsibility. Many external factors act upon us, but blaming them for *our* failures prevents us from getting to the root of the issue. The common denominator in all our decisions and actions is that *we* are participating in them. When we fail to take personal responsibility for the process, we present ourselves as victims of circumstance and damage our credibility. One of the surest ways to build credibility is to seek out opportunities to take responsibility and have a hand in righting wrongs. "When you act as a leader, you exercise control over your life; this will naturally influence and inspire those around you. Relinquishing control of your life to external situations, circumstances, and culture is the opposite."* Credibility is predicated on the ability to be flexible.

Flexibility

Stay committed to your decisions, but stay flexible in your approach.

—**Tom Robbins**

Change is inevitable, and is happening all around us every day. We naturally and intuitively try to reduce the complexities of an undertaking to fit into the framework created by our presuppositions and schemas about the way things are. This has the opposite effect by creating additional complexity in the long run. An anima-based leader understands the need to suspend those preconceptions in order to be open to alternative perspectives. This allows one to actually be open to the evolving challenges and variables of the mission. It has been said that when you cannot change a situation, you are forced to change yourself.

The profession of law enforcement is growing increasingly complex. Leaders need to challenge their own presuppositions on a continuous basis and learn to consider alternative perspectives. Failure to do so drastically limits one's ability to understand the real and felt needs of the community and be proactive in helping things go right. A leader must be flexible in his approach to problem solving and the allocation of the agency's resources. A person with strong character is principled; however, a paradox exists. A strong leader must be committed to personal and organizational values, but at the same time be open to new ideas and able to adapt to changing realities. Just as the flexibility of a joint can be increased by performing stretching exercises, flexibility in leadership can be increased by stretching one's mind to consider alternative perspectives, which can influence our thinking and guide us to unconventional but extremely effective solutions.

A rigid mind-set is self-limiting and self-deceiving. It produces false confidence when dealing with a familiar problem, but causes us to become overwhelmed when faced with challenges that are more ambiguous. Consider the widely misunderstood subject of police use of force. What constitutes reasonable force varies from situation to situation and is heavily dependent on context and an assortment of variables. This is probably the vaguest area

* Mark Sanborn, You Don't Need a Title to Be a Leader (Boulder, Colo.: WaterBrook Press, 2006), 33.

of a very indistinct profession. These considerations serve to challenge and perplex administrators. Most agencies have a use-of-force policy on the books, and many of those policies employ some type of matrix, model, or continuum that attempts to educate practitioners on balanced options for responding to resistance or aggression. The purpose of these "mechanical applications" is to assist training officers in teaching concepts concerning reasonableness as it relates to force application. The purposes of such matrices are not to "define" reasonableness, and it is dangerous to use them in this manner. Unfortunately, many supervisory personnel, when faced with the uncertainty that is inherent in use-of-force incidents, fall back on the use-of-force model as an evaluation tool to determine whether an officer acted reasonably. The supervisors who do this are not being maniacal; they are simply incapable of, or untrained in, adopting a flexible mind-set. Rigidity in the critical analysis process results in a complete breakdown of the decision-making process. Some of the results of failing to analyze a use-of-force incident in the proper context are as follows:

- Unwarranted discipline
- Lowering of morale
- Precipitation of improper hesitation on the part of officers involved in tense, uncertain, and rapidly evolving circumstances

The ability to be comfortable with ambiguity and flexible in response to challenges is a natural outcome of anima-based leadership. It is of chief importance that leaders utilize sound discretion when evaluating decisions made in rapidly evolving circumstances. We build our flexibility by constantly challenging ourselves to consider new and inventive ways to see problems and consider new solutions. When faced with challenges and opportunities in an uncertain environment, a leader utilizes creativity to arrive at unconventional solutions: "[T]he creative person is a risk taker, but carefully considers what could go wrong and is prepared to deal with the complications. The leader learns from failure and tries to understand the system that set a person up for error rather than looking for a scapegoat."*

Communication Skills

The single biggest problem in communication is the illusion that it has taken place.

—**George Bernard Shaw**

---

* Donald J. Palmisano, On Leadership-Essential Principles for Success (New York: Skyhorse Publishing, 2008), 118.

When recruits join the academy, they face a daunting curriculum list that must be mastered in order for them to earn the right to protect and serve their communities. Recruits receive instruction on everything from constitutional law to mechanics of arrest; from report writing to handcuffing; and from patrol procedures to cultural diversity training. One of the biggest gaps in this long list of training protocol is communication skills. Don't get me wrong: there are many courses out there labeled as "tactical communications" training, but most focus on only one side of the communications process—getting your point across to someone. In order for true communication to occur, true understanding must take place on the part of both participants in the conversation. This requires a communication system that is based on the premise of seeing others as they really are—as people, instead of objects to be manipulated within the framework of a call for service or weekly staff meeting.

The truth is that most of the shortcomings in the area of communication do not result from the participants' lack of desire. Almost everyone would agree that all relationships, professional and personal, would be greatly enhanced by improvement in this area of interpersonal relations. Most people want to be good at exchanging thoughts and ideas; they just lack the skill to get the job done. We have all sat through courses designed to teach us to diffuse domestic arguments, but how many officers have had training to help them deal with a superior on issues related to a question of integrity?

The KCPD Leadership Academy employs the CLEAR* model in communications training. While most models focus on selling someone on a suggestion or behavior, the CLEAR model is rooted in the idea that the person(s) you are speaking with have ideas and motivations that are just as important as your own, and they must be understood before you are capable of influencing them with the content of your message. The objective of this courageous communications model is to produce principled and collegial relationships that are rooted in integrity.

A leader must share the organization's message with direct reports. Communicating information to the people you supervise is one of the surest ways to demonstrate your care and compassion for them. I make it a practice to share as much information as possible with the men who report to me. When someone e-mails me about a decision or policy recommendation that has the potential to affect our squad, I always attempt to seek input from the troops. My squad executes high-risk search warrants on a daily basis. We travel together in, and deploy out of, a large passenger van that has been converted and specially outfitted to facilitate our job. As you can imagine, seven guys jumping in and out of a van wearing 70 lbs. of gear

---

* Gus Lee and Diane Elliott-Lee, Courage: The Backbone of Leadership (San Francisco: Jossey-Bass, 2006).

can take its toll on a vehicle. Captain Wadle, our unit commander, recently worked hard to get a new van ordered to replace the one we currently use because it was old and becoming a maintenance nightmare. When the new van arrived at the maintenance garage, I received a call from the fleet operations manager. He wanted me to stop by the garage and instruct the maintenance crew on how to outfit the new van. In our culture, the supervisor typically makes these types of decisions. The crew leader was surprised when I showed up with my entire squad. They spent the better part of an hour climbing in and out of the van and bouncing ideas around as the fleet personnel took notes and tried to keep up. I had my share of ideas and input; however, when it came time to leave the garage, the only idea of mine that made it into the final plan was that we should keep the van black. When I reflected back on the time we spent designing the layout of the van, I realized that I could not have come up with the best ideas on my own if I had been given a week to do it. Open, honest communication is a key component of getting the most for your effort in terms of inspiring ingenuity in others.

The act of communicating openly shows you care about the well-being of your people and trust them to understand and act on the information. When I use the term "your people," I do not mean to imply they somehow belong to you. Rather, as a leader, you are *responsible* for them and to them for achieving results that align with high core values and organizational priorities. Communication, trust, and accountability are the lifeblood of organizations. When leaders listen to others, they send the message that all viewpoints are valued, and it encourages everyone to become more involved in the organization's success. Remember, once a person feels understood, she is naturally influenced by the content of your message.

Trust

Whoever is careless with the truth in small matters cannot be trusted with the important matters.

—**Albert Einstein**

Trust is necessary for any leader who seeks to influence and inspire. It is very difficult to attain and all too simple to damage. The cultivation of trust in any team is not a simple process and must be expanded from the inside out. It begins with developing what leadership author Stephen M. R. Covey (the son of leadership great Stephen R. Covey) calls "self trust." "Self Trust deals with the confidence we have in ourselves—in our ability to set and achieve goals, to keep commitments, to walk our talk—and also with our ability to inspire trust in others."* We have to make and keep commitments to ourselves before we will be capable of honoring commitments we make to the people we serve. The ability to trust oneself is a foundational component of anima-based leadership. When you are certain you are able to make and keep commitments to yourself, it helps to reinforce your ability to hold others accountable for acting for what is right. After all, if you cannot trust yourself, how can you expect others to place their trust in you?

Trust is the foundation of teamwork, and law enforcement is definitely a team sport. When the team learns that the leader will follow through and do the things he promises, trust is grown and loyalty is increased exponentially. While opportunities to establish and build trust naturally arise, it is not enough to wait around for them. A leader must look for opportunities to grow trust by actively seeking out situations that put his character on display for others to see. Become proactive in searching for issues that affect the well-being and morale of the people you serve, and address them openly. If a policy or procedure has outlived its usefulness and is no longer practical or is excessively burdensome, work to amend or abolish it before it becomes a point of contention that can damage organizational trust. When someone approaches you to gossip about others, use that opportunity to stand up for those who are not present. This sends a powerful message about your anima and works to grow trust. A leader who seeks to build trust must hold herself accountable to the organization's rules and expectations. A good leader must be capable of being a good follower.

Consider the sergeant who is given an unpopular edict from his captain that he knows is going to be met with resentment from the line officers. Moreover, he doesn't agree with the policy as a matter of preference. When he presents the idea to his sector, he says something like "The captain said we have to follow this new policy, but I don't think it is the right thing to do, so we are not going to do it." The sergeant may think that by disregarding the captain's instructions he is just being practical and looking out for the troops, but this type of passive defiance erodes trust from the top down. One day the sergeant will turn around to find that his direct reports aren't doing the things *he* tells them to do because they don't think *his* rules have merit. The unsuspecting sergeant is likely to wonder where they got the idea that it was acceptable to not follow orders, not realizing he modeled that very behavior for them. One way to help build trust is by following the rules and holding yourself accountable for your actions.

A leader who aspires to build trust openly shares credit with others. The idea is that there is enough recognition and praise to go around, and by sharing it generously you send the message that you value the effort of others.

---

* Stephen M. R. Covey, The Speed of Trust: The One Thing That Changes Everything (New York: Free Press, 2006).

Some people think they have to hoard as much credit as possible because there is only so much to go around. Leadership sage Stephen R. Covey refers to this type of thinking as the "Scarcity Mentality." People who suffer from the Scarcity Mentality have a very difficult time allowing others to receive praise or recognition and often harbor resentment toward those who are successful. Covey advocates that leaders pursue what he calls the "Abundance Mentality." This Abundance Mentality "flows out of a deep inner sense of personal worth and security. It is the paradigm that there is plenty out there and enough to spare for everybody. It results in sharing of prestige, of recognition, of profits, of decision making. It opens possibility, options, alternatives, and creativity."*

Some leaders unintentionally work to undermine trust by engaging in efficient "management" tasks. The employee evaluation process utilized by many departments is one example. At our agency, employees are formally evaluated twice a year. They get a mid-evaluation, which is a general summary of their performance, which is followed by a yearly evaluation six months later. The yearly evaluation carries the most weight, and their salary increase is dependent upon a satisfactory rating. The process in and of itself can help a supervisor manage performance; however, it does little to inspire others to be their best selves and insidiously works to undermine trust. This system mandates that supervisors only meet with their direct reports twice a year to discuss performance. The unintended consequence is that months can go by before an employee gets critical feedback on job performance. Employee evaluations should be dynamic, fluid, and ongoing. Leaders who desire to build trust must give feedback on a daily basis, often holding short, informal sessions and conversations. People want to know how they are doing, and giving regular input can help them set goals and meet organizational objectives. A leader who is frequently among the troops will find many situations that offer teaching points to help both leader and subordinate improve their performance. If implemented in a way that inspires trust, any evaluation system includes a mechanism by which the employee can evaluate the leader. What better way to help leaders focus on service to others than feedback and input from those she serves?

Trust is a cornerstone of success. It is a key ingredient in the lifeblood of any organization, relationship, or family. In an interdependent profession like law enforcement, trust is critical to the achievement of an agency's basic mission. The responsibility for building, extending, and earning trusts falls on the leader. Brian Tracy, author of *Maximum Achievement*, wrote, "The

---

* Stephen R. Covey, The 7 Habits of Highly Effective People: Powerful Lessons in Personal Change (New York: Fireside, 1990).

glue that holds all relationships together, including the relationship between the leader and the led, is trust, and trust is based on integrity."*

Discipline

No evil propensity of the human heart is so powerful that it may not be subdued by discipline.

—Seneca

It requires great discipline to achieve the type of character that will sustain one for a lifetime. This doesn't simply happen. It is not something one is born with; it is something that must be developed as a product of an inner focus that results in a critical look at our outward actions. A person who seeks to develop her character must shed the contemporary notion that conflict is something to be avoided. Conflict is what helps to forge a strong system of personal values.

Self-discipline is a major component of the character construction process. A leader who desires to inspire her followers must first demonstrate her ability to live out the attributes of a strong character. Self-discipline is developed by making and keeping commitments to oneself. Once you have demonstrated consistency of purpose, you can begin modeling the desired behavior for those you seek to influence and motivate. Can you imagine attending a course on healthy eating only to find out the instructor is very obese as a result of a horrible diet? How about a parent who smokes three packs of cigarettes a day punishing his teenager for lighting up? This same type of hypocrisy is at work in a leader who demands things of her troops that she does not demand of himself.

When we set lofty goals for ourselves, they often manifest with a sense of abstraction. We say things like "I want to be a better leader," or "I want to get into better shape." There is nothing inherently wrong with wanting to improve in these critically important areas; however, there are critical behaviors that need to be identified that will get us to the top of the mountain that is change. Getting into better shape is a concept, not a behavior. It is a result of doing something, or many things, in pursuit of attaining an ideal. What lies between where you begin and where you end are many hours of focused behavior modification. This is where discipline lives. Discipline is what it takes to win the battle of mind over mattress when you need to get out of bed and exercise before starting the day. It allows us to identify and adhere

---

* Brian Tracy, Maximum Achievement: Strategies and Skills That Will Unlock Your Hidden Powers to Succeed (New York: Simon & Schuster, 1995).

to critical behaviors that will lead us to the realization of our goals. Discipline grants us the opportunity to practice behavioral strategies that are the seed-bed of lasting change. Discipline is the action component that is missing from so many of the best-laid plans. An idea, goal, or pursuit without the discipline to engage in an active change effort can be equated to trying to operate a high-performance automobile without putting fuel in the tank. The practice of self-discipline is just that—practice. You are practicing for the time when you must help guide others in the ways of discipline and lasting change. Through rigorous commitment to self-discipline, a leader develops the confidence needed to lead others. Most failures of leadership have their roots in inconsistencies within the leader as opposed to external factors that press upon him. The walls of self-discipline become stronger and more fortified as we develop consistency and keep the commitments we make to ourselves.

Knowledge

True knowledge exists in knowing that you know nothing.

—Socrates

An aspiring leader must commit herself to lifelong learning. It takes just a matter of a few years to become functionally irrelevant in your field if you allow your learning to stagnate. While many think of learning as something that has a beginning and an end, a leader with a strong anima knows that learning is a lifelong pursuit that permits her to constantly reevaluate and retest the paradigms that got her to this point.

John Kotter identified five critical mental habits that support lifelong learning in his groundbreaking book, *Leading Change*:

- *Risk taking*: Willingness to push oneself out of comfort zones
- *Humble self-reflection*: Honest assessment of successes and failures, especially the latter
- *Solicitation of opinions*: Aggressive collection of information and ideas from others
- *Careful listening*: Propensity to listen to others
- *Openness to new ideas*: Willingness to view life with an open mind*

As you peruse these habits, note that to develop and nurture them requires a great deal of confidence and maturity. Risk taking requires one to be comfortable with the notion that not all risks end in success. A leader committed

* John P. Kotter, Leading Change (Boston: Harvard Business Press, 1996).

to lifelong learning must come to grips with the fact that failure is a necessary part of the creative process. Setbacks should be not only expected, but also embraced as opportunities to grow your anima in ways that will dramatically increase the level of effectiveness you can achieve. Some of the best lessons come as a result of realizing a mistake. We have already discussed the important role that humility plays in the leadership process. Without the ability to reflect honestly upon our past triumphs and failures, learning becomes impossible. Too often our natural tendency toward self-deception allows us to make excuses for our missteps, effectively strangling the feedback loop necessary for true knowledge growth. This same self-deception permits us to overestimate our individual contribution to our successes while effectively ignoring the efforts of the people around us. When our anima is strong, we are capable of not only tolerating the opinions of others, but also actually seeking out input from various perspectives. We are capable of respectful consideration of differing ideas. A leader of this caliber actually places a high value on opinions that conflict with her own because she realizes the vast potential that is unleashed when she steps outside of the self-imposed limits of her viewpoint. When we listen to others with the intent to understand them instead of with the intent to make ourselves understood, we open our minds to perspectives that we are incapable of tapping with our own myopic view of reality. New ideas that blossom into great innovations often come from the most unlikely of sources, and a leader must arm herself with an open mind so the best ideas don't escape her scrutiny. This is the foundation for lifelong learning.

A final word on anima-based leadership: it is not for the weak of spirit. When Jack and I begin to talk to leaders about unconditional respect, they often associate the concept with soft behavior. Nothing could be further from the truth. In order to display unconditional respect for others, you must possess a stalwart inner way. That means you must constantly be developing the proper attitude, requisite knowledge, and technical skill in all aspects of police work. Without these attributes, you are likely to be motivated by fear. Consider that humans have five instinctual responses to fear or stress. These responses are not learned; they are preloaded onto our respective hard drives at birth. They are *fight*, *flight*, *freeze*, *submit*, and *posture*. We spend countless hours trying to overcome these instinctual responses by substituting them with proper training and motivation because they are unacceptable responses for police officers. The rules often tell us when we can fight. Fleeing, freezing, and submitting are culturally and practically unacceptable options for those charged with protecting others. The only instinctual option available to a leader who is unprepared and not properly trained and skilled is to posture, which simply means "acting" tough and capable in an attempt to mask your fear and intimidate others into backing down. This posturing is often displayed by police officers on the street who scream and curse at the subjects of police scrutiny. It is displayed by lead-ers who become easily frustrated and direct anger (more often than not in the form of veiled threats) at their subordinates. The simple fact is that, in order to have unconditional respect for others, a leader must not only pos-sess true compassion, but also be physically and mentally capable of deliver-ing violence against someone when it is needed to protect himself or defend others. You must *BE* tough and capable, or you risk defaulting to a "natu-ral instinct" response when faced with leadership decisions, regardless of whether they occur during combat or a personnel counseling session. This is the basis for anima-based leadership for all leaders, and is foundational for unleashing the power of unconditional respect into our organizations and communities.

You Disgust Me! Does It Matter?

6

The mouth may lie, alright, but the face it makes nonetheless tells the truth.

—Friedrich Nietzsche, German philosopher (1844–1900)[*]

Does law enforcement's own comforting and anesthetizing folklore unintentionally breed condescension and disgust toward the community? Are condescension and disgust communicated regardless of how one puts on a professional image and speaks professional words? When members of our communities experience condescension and contempt in their dealings with law enforcement members, do individuals naturally react with hostility and resentment? Do hostility and resentment spread from one member of our community to the next as experiences are shared and stories told? Do these feelings carry into the next contact with law enforcement and reinforce any condescending and contemptuous perspectives of the next officer? Does this create a vicious cycle relentlessly running below the surface of conscious thought? In this cycle, do law enforcement and community members mutually foster hostile attitudes, words, and behaviors in the other? Do these hostile attitudes constantly serve to excuse and reinforce each other? Does this cycle actually serve to invite the very attitudes and behaviors that both sides *say* they hate from the other side? Does this self-perpetuating process with "sides" create an environment that constantly serves to obstruct the most basic mission of law enforcement? If there is even a remote possibility that the answer to any of the above questions is "yes," should law enforcement care enough to make the changes necessary to break the cycle? (Refer to the "String of Perils" [Figure 1.1], and simply insert the above-captured perils.)

To forget one's purpose is the commonest form of stupidity.

—Friedrich Nietzsche[†]

---

[*] Friedrich Nietzsche, "The mouth may lie, alright, but ..." quoted in Robert Andrews, Mary Biggs, and Michael Seidel, eds., The Columbia World of Quotations (New York: Columbia University Press, 2006); also available at eNotes.com. 2006, http://www.enotes.com/famous-quotes/the-mouth-may-lie-alright-but-the-face-it-makes (accessed November 6, 2008).

[†] http://www.quotationspage.com/quote/9310.html (accessed November 6, 2008).

Sheep, Sheepdogs, Wolves, and Shepherds

There is much philosophical thought and conversation about police and their role within their communities. One illustration, popularized by retired Army Lieutenant Colonel Dave Grossman, depicts the police as sheepdogs and the public as sheep.* While Grossman's article is inspirational and not problematic on its own, I consistently hear convoluted logic that grows out of it. This convoluted logic cavalierly explains the "natural" tension between law enforcement and the members of the community. I am not saying that this sheep–sheepdog illustration is the *cause* of the problem I am identifying. I am simply showing how it, like so many otherwise useful concepts, gets sucked up into the vortex of self-deceived thinking.

At first glance, it seems obvious to cops: the sheep are helpless and clueless. They are generally incapable of violence. Sheep have two settings: graze and stampede. As a result, they must be snarled at, nipped at, growled at, and herded around for their own good. They don't like the vicious treatment, or the sheepdog, and the more the sheep resist the sheepdog, the more the sheepdog is duty-bound to snarl louder, growl louder, and bite harder until the dim-witted sheep respond. The more the sheepdog intimidates the sheep, the more the sheep dislike the sheepdog ... until the wolf comes. Then all the sheep try to line up behind the one sheepdog they have always hated. Arguably, the research and examples quoted in the first two chapters of this book destroy the belief that most people are incapable of violence. The reality is that given the proper social construct, almost anyone will use even unmerited violence against others and establish complete internal justification for doing so. Obviously, during emergency circumstances such as an active shooter the situation is tense, uncertain, and rapidly evolving. Absent the proper mind-set development and training to establish tactical awareness and responses, almost anyone—law enforcement and military personnel included—will engage in counterproductive behaviors when under extreme duress (refer back to the discussion in Chapter 4 regarding the unintended consequences of training and the Newhall, California, incident).†

The unintended consequences of adopting such a presupposition (i.e., that most people are sheep and are incapable of violence—and must be

---

* Lieutenant Colonel Dave Grossman (ret.), "On Sheep, Wolves, and Sheepdogs," http://mwk-works.com/onsheepwolvesandsheepdogs.html (accessed October 28, 2008). Grossman is also the author of On Killing: The Psychological Cost of Learning to Kill in War and Society (Boston: Back Bay Books, 1996).
† Chris B. Hankins, "The New Paradigm: Police Trends toward More Powerful Handguns and the Mental Aspects of Combat Survival and Training," Criminal Justice Institute School of Law Enforcement Supervision Session 24, November 8, 2004, http://www.cji.net/papers/HankinsChris.pdf.

aggressively herded for their own protection) are potentially dangerous in at least two ways.

First, assuming that people will only freeze or stampede during violence gives law enforcement a narrow set of options to present people during a pre–violent encounter awareness and training session. It would be akin to firefighters telling occupants of a building, "If the building catches on fire, we don't want you dim-witted sheep to stampede and hurt one another—so lock yourself in a room and wait for the 'professionals' to show up and rescue you." This is generally what citizens get told by law enforcement community interaction trainers in dealing with an active shooter. "Lock yourself in a room and wait for the professionals to show up." Imagine the carnage of people sitting frozen in a room waiting for the "professional" police or firefighters to show up and rescue them. In fact, one does not have to imagine: only read the newspaper to see the resulting carnage of people sitting frozen in a chair or crawling under a table to hide from a madman with a gun. The "active shooter" calmly goes from person to person, makes one last contemptuous comment, and shoots in cold blood, then reloads, moves to the next trembling body, and repeats the process. All the while, the people are doing exactly as told: *nothing but waiting for the professionals.* In many cases, law enforcement's presuppositions about the innate dysfunction of "sheep" in tense situations lead the "sheepdog" *and* the "sheep" astray. (Refer again to the string of perils illustration in Figure 1.1; again, simply insert new perils.) On the other hand, there have been examples of "victims" of active shooters stopping the violence. This is particularly important because most active-shooter situations are over in a few minutes, usually before professional law enforcement personnel arrive and deploy. The idea of a few terrorists with box knives being able to co-opt a commercial airliner full of people into a manned missile is a thing of the past. Before the first two planes hit on 9/11, the conventional wisdom (from law enforcement) was to cooperate with the hijackers, sit still, and let the professionals handle it after landing. Within minutes of the first two planes hitting, the "sheep" on another commercial airliner changed the rules forever. They forced the hijackers to crash their would-be guided missile into the ground. Why would law enforcement wish to maintain presuppositions that have the unintentional result of giving active shooters the ability to unleash their carnage with impunity for several seemingly unending minutes until the professionals arrive?

Second, why does law enforcement continually find itself in the role of snarling at an unwilling public? Maybe it is *because* law enforcement often snarls and herds, rather than leads, strengthens, and encourages. Maybe it's because law enforcement has taken the easy, ego-stroking way out, and forgone timeless principles of policing. Maybe something that should be a *tool* in the hands of law enforcement, the ever-loyal sheepdog, has become the permanent *persona* of choice (again, see the string of perils). Take current active shooter training as an example of a *tool or temporary persona*. Here is my personal recap of current KCPD active shooter training:

> Officers are trained to lay aside old paradigms of officer safety (take cover and set up a perimeter—like in Columbine) and rather enter the building with guns drawn and pointed downrange. Officers move rapidly toward the gun-fire—closing swiftly on the shooter. Officers advance relentlessly, exchanging gunfire to eliminate the threat. If one officer falls, another fills in the line and the advance continues to eliminate the threat. Officers ignore fleeing citizens (even injured ones) with a singular focus on the threat.

It is easy to see that this presents an entirely different persona to a student in a school than a typical school resource officer should present on an average day. For those few intense minutes, the officer must become a relentless predator: rapidly moving, focused, and intense. While this is the only appropriate response for the situation, many seem to have made what should be a law enforcement avatar (a temporary manifestation or aspect of a continuing entity)* a permanent persona. I should note here that this "temporary manifestation of a continuing entity" is nonetheless *deeply rooted in the anima we are advocating*. To an outside observer, the officer will "look" and "act" completely different for those few moments. If the observer did not know the context (closing in on an active shooter who is slaughtering innocent children), he may even feel the officer is being rude or callous by ignoring the fleeing or injured students she passes by with seemingly no regard. Only the *context* can determine if a behavior is honoring or dishonoring, or respectful or disrespectful. *Most* behaviors separated from the context are impossible to evaluate. Relentlessly pursuing and shooting an active shooter who is slaughtering innocent children comprise the pinnacle of righteousness of action. This action (like every time an officer uses force) should be devoid of inappropriate hesitation and delivered with as much professionalism, vigor, and skill as the officer can muster.

Now back to the problem at hand: allowing what should be a "temporary manifestation" to become a permanent persona of choice. Maybe this persona has been adopted because personal anima rooted in integrity, buttressed by courage, and expressed as unconditional respect for all is hard work and therefore has been abandoned.

If one insists on the shepherding motif, I would propose the model of the *shepherd* rather than the sheepdog—in particular, the good Near Eastern shepherd who tenderly cares for the sheep, leads the sheep, and yet would ferociously guard the sheep with reckless abandon for his or her own safety.

---

* American Heritage Dictionary of the English Language, rev. 4th ed. (New York: Houghton Mifflin, 2003); see also http://www.thefreedictionary.com/avatar (accessed November 28, 2008).

So effective is the shepherd that he or she need not snarl and nip; the sheep recognize the sound of the good shepherd's voice and clamor to follow closely, in good times and bad.

Cared for in this manner, the sheep can actually be encouraged to "police" their own ranks, to release their focus on the snarling sheepdog long enough to expose the wolf in their ranks and take responsibility for their own safety. This is the essence of partnering with the community (and I argue that this is the basic mission of law enforcement). Once law enforcement has accomplished its basic mission, the community is enabled to unite with law enforcement in their *joint* basic mission: instilling safety, security, and prosperity within the fold. If these principles and outcomes sound vaguely familiar, it's because they are based on Sir Robert Peel's timeless principles of policing.

A great example of this in action occurred right here in Kansas City, Missouri. Kansas City's Westside had been a vibrant ethnic community for decades. But during the 1990s and into the early 2000s, Kansas City was being inundated with hundreds of undocumented people. Many of these people settled into or moved through the Westside. A large group would gather at the corner of Southwest Boulevard and Summit Street, a site that had long been the unofficial gathering place of day laborers awaiting employment. But with a liquor store at the intersection and the number of gathering men quadrupling, it became a breeding ground for all sorts of crime and problems. Traditional law enforcement responses of zero tolerance (growl, snarl, and nip) not only did not work to curb troubling behavior and crime but also—because the sheep circled and cowered, focused on the sheepdogs—gave the few wolves among the sheep the ability to hide within the fold and wreak havoc. Zero tolerance also brought cries of civil rights violations and angry pushback from community leaders. Yet being laissez-faire brought cries from the community that police were disregarding and "snubbing" them. It was only when law enforcement stepped back from their sheepdog role, went to the community, and really listened to understand the issue from the perspectives of all the stakeholders (i.e., build partnerships) that lasting solutions and effective responses were discovered. As a result, crime went down; problematic undocumented persons were identified and dealt with decisively; the sheep, no longer cowering at the snarling sheepdog, began to police their own ranks; and quality of life was vastly improved for all the stakeholders.*

---

* Kansas City (Mo.) Chief of Police James Corwin, "Day Laborers: Improving the Quality of Life for Laborers, Employers, and Neighbors," The Police Chief 73, no. 4 (April 2006): http://www.policechiefmagazine.org/magazine/index.cfm?fuseaction=print_display&article_id=862&issue_id=42006 (accessed November 1, 2008).

Here is a unique perspective on the Westside CAN (Community Action Center). Officer Octavio Villalobos grew up on the Westside and is now a Kansas City officer who works the Westside CAN.

I grew up on the Westside. The neighborhood was divided by Southwest Blvd. into a north and south end. On the corner of Southwest Blvd. and summit was a liquor store that was dubbed a grocery store. The liquor store was also where the many undocumented immigrant workers congregated, waiting for work. When I was a young boy, I remember there being as many as fifty men standing around, some panhandling, and others drunk. I remember being scared because they knew I had money going into the store and food coming out. I had to cross this gauntlet daily to get to the community center to participate in Boy Scouts or sports. I remember them cat-calling my mom. I distinctly remember the smell of urine and feces. They were not allowed to use the local business's restrooms, so it wasn't uncommon for pedestrians to see these guys popping a squat behind a building or urinating out in the open. Many restaurants and businesses struggled to maintain loyal customers due to the environment these men created. Criminals were able to survive within this group. Business owners who called the police were threatened. The community did not have faith in the PD and felt helpless to the point that they just accepted the situation.

I left the Westside to go to the army. I came back and eventually moved out of the Westside. I became a police officer and came back sometime after the Westside CAN established the day laborers initiative. Almost instantly, the businesses started thriving. New businesses opened, including the community's first-ever bank. All I could do was be grateful to Police Officer Matthew Tomasic and Linda Callon (the civilian director of the Westside CAN) because I knew that the days of mothers and their children having to walk through that situation, that smell, that gauntlet, were over. The community became partners with the police through the CAN center. The community's trust in our department was restored after many, many years of distrust. Longtime residents like Rosa (see the second vignette by Officer Villalobos on page 90) saw their neighborhood thrive as crime in that area decreased. They observed officers working *with* the community and being inclusive in the process. The officers express interest, display concern, and act with compassion. I felt proud, as an officer, of the message that was being sent to my community by my fellow officers. The community constantly reminds the KCPD of their concern for the lack of Latino representation on the police department. The CAN officer's willingness to work hard and with the community helped the police department send an important message. Any officer, regardless of race, can succeed in a community as long as they are invested in the people of that community and find ways to work with and have an inclusive approach to dealing with the community's issues. Each officer has the power and ability, if he or she chooses to, to send the message that he or she cares.

Leading Ourselves Astray

There is a real sense in which we are all like sheep and are easily led astray by our social identification clan (see Chapter 1). The sheep–sheepdog analogy could be one of those examples:

- When law enforcement is led astray and encouraged to assume the role of a snarling, contemptuous dog
- When law enforcement is anesthetized into believing that the effect that snarling has on the community *is the community's fault* because they are being like the dim-witted sheep they are

One could easily conclude that many in law enforcement have traded its noble birthright as the guardian class for a bowl of stew. This stew contains the "meat" that appeals to one's basest nature of being a despot, and it contains the aroma that intoxicates with the self-deception of blaming others for the consequences of our most offensive actions. All the while, law enforcement is abandoning its basic mission—partnering with our community—thus cutting off the various sections and individuals of the community at large that are to partner with law enforcement.

The "Face" of Self-Deception

There are many other presuppositions that would cause law enforcement to build misconceptions and lead us astray. Take, for example, the misconception that one can hold any disrespectful, contemptuous internal attitude toward others as long as he puts on a professional face and uses professional language. Current research has exploded that anesthetizing myth: as Dr. Donald Nathanson, executive director of the Silvan S. Tomkins Institute, and clinical professor of psychiatry and human behavior at Jefferson Medical College, explained while giving a report to the Academic Advisory Council of the National Campaign against Youth Violence, "In general, affects [physiological mechanisms that underlie all emotion] are expressed on the display board of the face long before they are experienced anywhere else."* In other words, the affect we experience when dealing with others

---

* "The Name of the Game Is Shame," Jefferson Medical College report to the Academic Advisory Council of the National Campaign against Youth Violence (first distributed December 2000 and presented in part at the Secret Service Building in Washington, D.C.), current rev. March 2003, http://www.tomkins.org/PDF/library/articles/thenameofthe-gameisshame.pdf (accessed October 28, 2008).

is expressed on our faces before we *consciously* experience the affect in our own emotions.

- Fact: we *will* display the affects of disgust and anger on our face automatically.

The implications of Nathanson's work give a research basis for a philosophical position that has a very similar implication. According to Dr. C. Terry Warner, "By seeing others suspiciously, accusingly or fearfully we *become* suspicious, accusing, or fearful ourselves.... *The kind of people we are cannot be separated from how we interpret the world around us.*"*

Restating the self-deceiving falsehood and fact:

- Falsehood: one can harbor an internal attitude of disgust or anger toward others but effectively mask it with professional language and actions.
- Fact: an internal anima that holds others as disgusting is automatically and instantly flashed across the face.

Self-Deception Unmasked

"Well, maybe we can get away with it; maybe the dim-witted sheep won't pick up on our flashes of disgust." As we illustrated above, the research is overwhelmingly against this type of wishful thinking. In average healthy people, a specific region of the brain, saturated with neurons, is utilized for the recognition of faces and facial expressions.[†] In keeping with this, research consistently finds when asking "how quickly perceivers could recognize expressions of anger, contempt, disgust, embarrassment, fear, happiness, pride, sadness, shame, and surprise" that "[a]cross both studies, perceivers quickly and efficiently ... recognized most emotion expressions."[‡] This article, "The Automaticity of Emotion Recognition," also notes compelling evidence that emotional expressions are cross-culturally recognized and that people will physically react to subliminal expressions without even being consciously aware of it.[§] To make matters worse for law enforcement,

---

* C. Terry Warner, Bonds That Make Us Free: Healing Our Relationships, Coming to Ourselves (Salt Lake City, Utah: Shadow Mountain Press, 2001), 41 (italics in original).
† Nancy Kanwisher, Josh McDermott, and Marvin M. Chun, "The Fusiform Face Area: A Module in Human Extrastriate Cortex Specialized for Face Perception," Journal of Neuroscience 17, no. 11 (June 1, 1997): 4302–11. Copyright ©1997 Society for Neuroscience, http://www.jneurosci.org/cgi/content/abstract/17/11/4302.
‡ J. L. Tracy and R. W. Robins, "The Automaticity of Emotion Recognition," University of British Columbia, Department of Psychology, Emotion and Self Lab, http://ubc-emotion-lab.ca/wp-content/images/2008/02/automaticity-emotion-2008.pdf (accessed September 9, 2009.
§ Tracy and Robins, "The Automaticity of Emotion Recognition."

other research concludes that when we deal with others we consider as being higher than ourselves on a social hierarchy (such as a citizen dealing with an officer), our brain lights up with resources to read, interpret, and respond to the other person: "viewing a superior individual differentially engaged perceptual-attentional, saliency, and cognitive systems."[*]

To add to the previously made points:

- Fact: almost everyone who law enforcement deals with is uniquely suited to and intrinsically dynamic in reading many facial expressions, including anger and disgust.

The Price of Self-Deception

If you were to ask two attorneys who have been highly successful at suing doctors, "How do you pick your targets?" or "Why do doctors get sued?" you would get a definite, unambiguous answer from both of them. This answer ought to send chills down the spine of anyone in law enforcement clinging to this previously stated falsehood (i.e., that one can harbor an internal attitude of disgust or anger toward others but effectively mask it with professional language and actions) and who has any compunction regarding the basic mission of law enforcement to build *partnership* with our communities.

People don't sue doctors who make mistakes. People sue doctors who make mistakes *and*:

- are arrogant
- are condescending
- don't treat patients with respect
- don't establish a relationship
- don't apologize for mistakes[†]

Does this apply to law enforcement?

Consider the issue from the perspective of Sergeant DeEtta Jacobs. She is (as of early 2009) a supervisor in the Kansas City Police Department's Internal Affairs Unit and has overseen and reviewed over 400 investigations into citizen complaints.

---

[*] Caroline F. Zink, Yunxia Tong, Qiang Chen, Danielle S. Bassett, Jason L. Stein, and Andreas Meyer-Lindenberg, "Know Your Place: Neural Processing of Social Hierarchy in Humans," Cell Press, Neuron Article (2008): 1.

[†] American Association of Neurological Surgeons, "How Plaintiffs' Lawyers Pick Their Targets," AANS.org, http://www.aans.org/library/Article.aspx?ArticleId=10046 (accessed November 1, 2008).

I have been with the department since February 10, 1986. I started as a DFO, went to the academy January 20, 1987, and graduated June 14, 1987. I have worked every patrol division with the exception of South Patrol Division, two tours in Detention, Personnel Employment, Property and Evidence, Drug Enforcement and Internal Affairs. I have been a sergeant with the department for sixteen years. I have been assigned to Internal Affairs for three years (January 2006–present). Our office receives an average of 280–300 complaints per year for investigation; of those I review half, so in three years I would have reviewed approximately 420–450 citizen complaint files. In addition, I have reviewed approximately 24 internal investigations during that same period.

During an investigation the complainant's formal statement is taken, any witnesses identified by the complainant are interviewed, and statements are taken if applicable. The detective conducts an area canvass to identify any additional witnesses to the reported event and to determine the possibility of video footage from private sources such as store surveillance cameras, both inside and out. The detective will interview neighbors and patrons to determine who may have information. It is during this gathering that rudeness and discourtesy are most often noted. There are many times when a witness will report the citizen's poor behavior and the officer's professional response; however, there are times when those same witnesses will report they could understand the officer needing to go hands-on, but they sure didn't like the way the officer talked to the suspect/complainant/citizen. Family members are particularly sensitive to the tones and demeanor used with their loved ones.

There are occasions when the complainant cannot articulate exactly what it was or how the officer spoke, but they felt disrespected. It is hard to document and it is hard to counsel someone on tone and body language without vivid video because the officer falls back on the words used. Voice inflection, disdain, and lack of care or concern are readily picked up in an officer's voice, especially when the citizen is looking for it. As noted above, many passive witnesses accept officers needing to go hands-on, as long as it is reasonable, but those same witnesses will not accept rude or demeaning treatment. If the officer treats the arrestee with respect when the physical encounter is over the witnesses often report the arrest[ee] got what he deserved. However, if the officer is condescending, mocking, or rude the support of the witnesses is not there.

The officers with a masked approach generally have more confrontations and complaints. Our primitive selves have been trained throughout evolution to read the body language of others, most often subconsciously, to evaluate and size up each other. Just because I smile and use nice words does not mean I cannot convey utter contempt; it's in the eyes and the tone.

In conclusion, yes, my experience does support the premise that contempt cannot be effectively hidden during police–citizen interaction. If the behavior is captured on audio or video, complaints have been sustained for rudeness, i.e., a traffic officer who ends his contact with a sarcastic "Have a nice day." The voice inflection and body language are hard for citizens to describe, and sometimes they don't know what it was, but they know they were treated rudely. I have also found that contempt breeds contempt. When the officer is contemptuous or condescending, the citizen mirrors the behavior. That type of behavior also tends to elicit more third-party complaints.

For more anecdotal accounts, while working on this chapter, we had a gathering at our home. The conversation came around to where one of the sweetest young mothers I know told me about being brought to tears after being stopped and condescendingly scolded by an officer (in a different jurisdiction). The image that came to mind was of an uncontrollably angry parent scolding a child or a master scolding a dog. It reminded me of one time when I was stopped, *while in uniform*, driving home from working the night shift. I don't know what the KCPD officer's name was, but I know he has long since retired. I watched in my mirror as he unsnapped his revolver and pulled it half out of his holster before approaching my vehicle. Even after seeing that I was a fellow officer and *acknowledging that I had not broken any traffic laws*, he still proceeded to scold me because he felt that the way I drove past him had "disrespected" him as an officer. The phrase we use is *contempt of cop*. Many fights and questionable arrests have been made for this "offense." How do you think that I, as a young cop who worked the inner city, reacted to this seasoned suburban cop scolding me? I shudder to think about how this situation would have left me seething with anger and contempt three or four years earlier when I was a 19-year-old kid. Is the self-fulfilling iterative process involved with internal hostility painfully obvious, or is it just me? I am not trying to pile it on; I am trying to express the generally ignored gravity of the situation and the *long-term costs involved*.

Admittedly, if policies are reasonably followed, an officer will rarely face monetary loss or even discipline for being *perceived* as condescending, disrespectful, or rude toward members of the community. That is not the cost I am referring to. I am referring to the fact that on-duty officers are generally outnumbered by members of the community by a ratio of thousands to one; the burning need to partner with the community becomes painfully obvious. *Every contact with every member of the community must be seen as an opportunity to build partnership.* Condescending, contemptuous, and disrespectful attitudes on the part of law enforcement members poison interactions and create a bunker mentality in the minds of citizens. Citizen bunker mentality creates a "self-fulfilling prophecy" that affirms and hardens the contemptuousness of law enforcement. Common observation tells us that people will repeatedly tell the same story of mistreatment to everyone they know and whoever will listen—so no one event happens in isolation to the whole of public perception. Consider another account from Officer Octavio Villalobos regarding the efforts of the Westside CAN with a lady we will call Rosa.

Rosa used to be a volunteer at the CAN center. She's a 60+-year-old respected and influential member of the Westside community. For a long time, she did not trust police officers because of past negative experiences between officers and the residents of the Westside community. Rosa's trust in the KCPD was restored by PO Tomasic and his past CAN partners. She witnessed how these officers began to address the issues in her community through inclusive initiatives and visible compassion for the members of her community. She eventually began to offer her time answering phones and doing other things to help around the CAN center because she believed in the work of the officers. The officers were grateful for her help and always tried to encourage all community members to participate in calling the police and reporting crime. One day, Rosa became involved in a confrontation with a neighbor wielding a knife and expressing hostility toward her. Rosa contacted the CAN officers on their personal phones. Unfortunately, the officers were not working on that day but encouraged Rosa to contact the police and assured her that the officers that worked her area would respond and handle the situation. Rosa was skeptical about dealing with officers she didn't know but dialed 911 to report the situation anyway. Upon arriving on the scene, the officer first made contact with the suspect, who was able to convince the officer that nothing was going on and that Rosa was just a nosy old lady. When Rosa saw the officer outside, she came out of her house and tried to tell the officer that the suspect was armed and explain to him that she was the one who called 911. Using "command presence," the officer yelled at Rosa and told her to go back inside the house. Rosa was frightened and told the CAN officers that the officer was intimidating and never cared to ask her side of the story. She told the officers that this is the way it always has been and she felt foolish for thinking that times have changed. Since the incident, Rosa has quit coming to the CAN center and has told the officers of the CAN center that it was very hard to go through that and at this time, she was not ready to trust the police department. She was very hurt and disappointed. Although the officer never violated any policy, his attitude gave Rosa the impression that he did not care and she was not important enough for him to listen to. Rosa immediately assumed that it was because of what she looked like and where she lived that caused the officer to act this way toward her. I've witnessed numerous times officers treating victims this way, almost without conscious intent, as if to say, "Why are you bothering me? It's your fault for living in this area."

I could give numerous examples of this reality, but oddly enough, just today while in the middle of writing this chapter, I had a chance encounter with a man in his early fifties who had been a lifetime Kansas City resident. When this man realized I was a police officer, he began talking fondly of his brother-in-law, who used to be a police officer in another state, and other officers he has known. His demeanor was open and supportive as he talked. At this point, our conversation turned to a particular officer who had been killed in the line of duty nearly three decades ago. This man's countenance and demeanor instantly changed. He became tense and tight-jawed. The man asked if I knew the officer personally (which I did not), and then he proceeded to go on a tirade against this officer. The man said that when he was a high school kid, this officer patrolled the district that he lived in. He said that the officer was mean and pushy. The man went on for a few minutes, using all kinds of expletives against the officer even to the point of saying that when he heard the officer was killed, he was glad. I explained to the man that during the late 1960s–early 1970s era, many in law enforcement had an "us-versus-them" mentality because there was a huge cultural shift taking place along with accompanying civil unrest. The demeanor and attitude of the officer in question were probably "caught" from some of his peers and maybe even his trainers. The man then began to apologize for talking badly about a deceased officer and became somewhat remorseful (he really seemed like a kind and thoughtful man). I told the man that the unfortunate thing is that when one officer treats people poorly, the people carry the frustration of that into their next interaction with the next officer. If the next officer was not predisposed to be rude or abrasive, certainly he could become so if the citizen has a hostile attitude based on the interaction with the last officer. I told the man that breaking this cycle is one of the things that I teach at the academy. The man responded that if we were able to teach officers to break that cycle, no one could ever estimate how much that would benefit the police department and the community. I obviously agree. This account is amazing and instructive to the discussion. It profoundly illustrates the power of police demeanor to impact a person's internal attitude almost thirty years later.

I do not wish to paint with too broad a brush here; on the other hand, take my dad as an example. My dad has lived in Kansas City since shortly after retiring from the Navy some forty years ago. To my recollection, he has had formal contact with the police about once every ten to fifteen years over the last forty years (by making a report of some type). My dad has spoken about the quality of those contacts to almost everyone he knows. Before his son became an officer, those contacts became *the* lens though which my dad evaluated every story or news report about the police he heard. And those few contacts shaped every conversation he had about the police. My dad has always supported the police with every opportunity he had.

Sowing and Reaping

I suppose the principle behind sowing and reaping has been taught since people began to farm. It's a simple but profound concept. What one sows (green beans or peas), one can logically expect to reap in kind (green beans or peas).

The current research on brain–mind functionality that has been *briefly* summarized within this book supports this principle. The concept has been honed and expanded with social research. For example, the "Pygmalion effect" holds that our preconceived notions about people dictate what we sow into their lives and that this greatly influences what is reaped.*

The concept has been honed and expanded within the study of philosophy, to paraphrase the Arbinger Institute: every person has needs, fears, hopes, and concerns. When I disregard or minimize the needs, fears, and concerns of others, I see them as less than human, or as objects. To see another person as an inferior object is to do violence toward his or her personhood. Without fail, I will communicate my violence toward his or her personhood. Without fail, others will detect and react to my violence toward their personhood. The other's reaction will elicit more violence from me, and the cycle will continue to erode the quality and effectiveness of our interaction.†

The New Testament makes much of this principle of sowing and reaping (see 2 Corinthians 9:6 and Galatians 6:7–8), and our daily life experience presses the reality of this principle upon us.

How, then, do we tend to ignore or be blind to the sowing-and-reaping cycle of attitudes we breed and allow within law enforcement? How do we generally manage to blame the "other side" when we reap distrust, diminished cooperation, and silos and cycles of *omerta*, both within our organizations and from the community? The answer seems clear: *it's the easiest and most natural way to be.* Blaming others to justify my attitudes and actions is simple and instinctive. When others react to my attitudes and actions, their behavior creates a self-fulfilling feedback loop to justify my original attitudes and actions (see the "inverted asshole theory" and explanation in Chapter 2). On the other hand, in order to reap an intensely loyal, supportive, and engaged community whose creative energies and courageous actions are unleashed around the joint basic mission of instilling safety, security, and prosperity within the community, law enforcement must do the following: model, teach, and have enforced systems of feedback and accountability around a personal anima that sees all people as people and is rooted in integrity, buttressed by courage, and expressed in unconditional respect for all. This is *relentlessly hard work* both on an individual and on an organizational level. If I adopt this anima, then I have no one to blame for my attitudes, words, and actions but myself, so it is *unnatural and uncomfortable.*

The final chapter of this book will begin to explain a process for implementation, providing a construct of how this could work and what it would look like. But it all starts with personal accountability and honesty about one's inner way toward others—anima.

---

* Robert Rosenthal and Lenore Jacobson, Pygmalion in the Classroom: Teacher Expectation and Pupils' Intellectual Development (Carmarthen, Wales: Crown House, 2003).
† Arbinger Institute, "The Arbinger Principles of Nonviolence," http://www.arbinger.com/downloads/principles_of_non_violence.pdf (accessed July 22, 2008).

From Noble Peace Officers to 911 Reactionary Force

7

Technological progress has merely provided us with more efficient means for going backwards.

—Aldous Huxley*

Those who choose to spend their time reacting to what has gone wrong are doomed to spend all their time reacting to what has gone wrong.

First, to state and solidify some basic presuppositions that run through this book:

- The basic mission of law enforcement (LE) is to build partnership with our communities and to leverage that partnership to promote safety, security, and prosperity within our communities and organization.
- Every LE contact with a community member *will* build, support, and promote OR destroy, oppose, and undermine both missions.
- When officers use force, which they will, it should be the pinnacle of righteous behavior. It should be devoid of improper hesitation, and contain all the professionalism, skill, and vigor the officer is capable of producing. Please do not see the use of kinetic force as the only or preferable tactic to subdue an opponent.

Tactics of Regard

Arising from our advocated anima in stillness is wisdom—and in activity is potency and influence.

At first, through preparation, conditioning, and skill development, competence in *combat rooted in force* is established. Then, ever so slowly, an increasing competence with *tactics rooted in regard* emerges.

Employing tactics of regard decimates the opponent's will to fight—but his body remains intact. He yields without battle through one of two general ways. The first and most desirable is to divert his attention from his uncompromising

---

* Brainy Quote, http://www.brainyquote.com/quotes/quotes/a/aldoushuxl101185.html (accessed November 13, 2008).

position. He finds the concerns and desires that founded his position are under-stood and satiated (this is most desirable because it produces an ally where there had been an adversary). The second is that in a state of dissonance, confusion, and bewilderment (*kuzushi*, or broken balance), he unequivocally submits.

These are called *tactics of regard* because they are realized only by hav-ing unconditional respect *and* regard for the humanity of your opponent, by understanding her as a person and as an individual. Then, you wisely utilize this understanding (intelligence) to reach a mutually beneficial conclusion (she is treated with dignity and respect, she is not embarrassed or injured, and justice is served).

It may be helpful to consider this from a different paradigm. Retired California Highway Patrol officer, attorney, and risk management expert Gordon Graham likes to paraphrase his favorite risk management guru, Archand Zeller:

> During the period of recorded history, there is little evidence to indicate that man has changed in any major respect. Because the man does not change, the kinds of errors he commits remain constant. *The errors that he will make can be predicted from the errors he has made.** (Emphasis in original)

Here lies a great paradox. An individual's private memories, fears, preju-dices, and schemas make his response to spontaneous situations unpredict-able. But at the same time, to those with astute regard for the humanity of others, there arises an intensely comprehensive strategic awareness. Now, the complacency, hubris, avarice, fear, self-centeredness, bias, attention limits, and distractibility (CHAFSBAD) of the opponent make the errors he will make while *acting out his unpredictability*, well—*predictable*.

Summary: the anima warrior's placid wisdom allows him to under-stand the opponent's CHAFSBAD without reacting to and being emotionally swamped by his own. The anima warrior will intuitively know when the oppo-nent's mental balance (*kuzushi*) has been broken. At this point, a wisely placed strategic twist (*nage-waza*) combined with the opponent's mental and emo-tional momentum make one of the two previously described outcomes easily attainable. Refer back to the example of the angry, screaming lady in Chapter 3 for a brief example of how tactics of regard can diffuse a volatile situation.

For the righteous use of kinetic force and "tactics of regard" to occur:

- Each member of an LE organization must be selected, hired, trained, and accountable to possess and relentlessly develop a personal anima

* Gordon Graham, speaker, Interagency Helicopter Managers Workshop: Continued Professional Training, March 14, 2003, http://www.wildfirelessons.net/documents/GG_OrgRM.pdf (accessed August 15, 2009).

that is rooted in integrity, buttressed by courage, and expressed as unconditional respect for all persons.
- The organization must have systems, hierarchical structures, and policies that support acting for what is right without regard for biases, fears, political correctness, loyalties, and the like.
- The organization must create and relentlessly maintain a social environment that encourages and supports everyone, and holds *everyone* (top to bottom) accountable, for the results enumerated above.

This will *animat*e the culture of both the organization and its community. It will produce the following:

- Members who are tactically alert and responsive to others in a manner that transfers to any environment, thus fostering emotional, psychological, and social well-being
- Safe, open, and honest communication that is respectful of differing opinions and results in better ideas for the organization and community
- A social contract that establishes a high-trust, low-stress environment where members blossom to be their best selves
- Clear, concise, and compelling purposes, goals, priorities, and polices that are seamlessly linked and aligned with the actual operating goals and policies of the organization
- A workforce and community whose creative energies and massive resources are melded together, producing synergy and exponential results around their joint basic mission

I know that many will bristle at several of these presuppositions, and I have heard the countercharge "We are a paramilitary organization, not a group of soft social workers!" What usually follow are anecdotal accounts (war stories) that one uses to justify his own lack of integrity, courage, character, and respect for others. The justifier generally picks out the most reprehensible or unintelligent examples of human behavior he knows of and uses it to buttress his own personal justifications.

There is much *insincerity* or *ignorance* contained in arguing the paramilitary concept as justification for seeing and treating people as objects. The *insincerity* is rooted in the lack of integrity and in the self-deception regarding one's own character. We have covered these issues in previous chapters, particularly Chapter 6, so I won't return to those now. The *ignorance* involved in this statement contains great irony. The irony is that the U.S. military under General David Petraeus has co-opted the noble birthright that law enforcement has in so many ways abandoned. The military has come to understand that underlying *any* insurgencies' ability to function within a geographic area, there *must* exist ethnographic, cultural, social, historical, anthropological, and economic realities to sustain and support its operation.* The same is true in any community. Simple observation and common sense tell us that some communities sustain pervasive criminal and gang activity and some do not. It is that simple. *I am not saying that members of the community intentionally support criminal activity. I am saying that supporting rampant criminal activity is the unintended consequences of many complex realities within the community.* I am also saying that it is the responsibility of law enforcement to have the character, wisdom, and patience to learn and understand what these complex realities are, and then to work with the community to thwart them. I think officers intuitively know which communities support criminal activity, and which do not. Just observe where most officers (particularly those with families) choose to live. I also think that this proposition is obvious through simple observation of real communities. One could revisit the Westside CAN story (in Chapter 6) as an example of law enforcement learning to understand and thwart complex realities that supported a culture of crime and despair. I am not saying that perpetrators of neighborhood crime and violence are equivalent by strict definition to insurgents in Iraq or Afghanistan. However, even in Iraq and Afghanistan, the line between a common outlaw and an insurgent is often blurred.† Recently, retired Army Lt. Col. Ivan Welch visited our Leadership Academy and conducted a seminar on counterinsurgency (COIN) work. Col. Welch utilized the same material used in COIN School in Iraq by the U.S. Army. Seated next to me was Linda Callon, who manages the Westside CAN. Linda and I listen intently and then agreed that the COIN playbook has an uncanny resemblance to what the Westside CAN did in Kansas City. In an article about Jesse James, Peter Kunkel, the former acting assistant secretary of the U.S. Army (Financial Management and Comptroller), makes the connection between Jesse James in post–Civil War Missouri and insurgents in Afghanistan and Iraq. Some saw James as an insurgent; others saw James as a common outlaw.‡ Regardless of how one evaluates people like James, the prize of large sums of cash—that motivated outlaws and insurgents to commit violent crimes—was practically eliminated by the advent of banking systems that removed the need to carry and store cash. This is obviously what the military would call a

---

* Dr. Jacob Kipp, Lester Grau, Karl Prinslow, and Captain Don Smith, "The Human Terrain System: A CORDS for the 21st Century," The US Army Professional Writing Collection, http://www.army.mil/professionalwriting/volumes/volume4/december_2006/12_06_2. html (accessed November 13, 2008).

† Peter E. Kunkel, "How Jesse James, the Telegraph, and the Federal Reserve Act of 1913 Can Help the Army Win the War on Terrorism: The Unrealized Strategic Effects of a Cashless Battlefield," The US Army Professional Writing Collection, http://www.army. mil/professionalwriting/volumes/volume6/december_2008/12_08_3.html (accessed December 22, 2008).

‡ Kunkel, "How Jesse James."

nonkinetic solution to very violent, often repeated crimes, or what one might call a tactic of regard. Military strategists are attempting to develop lessons learned from the mid-1800s in Missouri to Iraq and Afghanistan today. This concept should also serve as a lesson learned for police and their communities today. I am *not* referring to the *exact* application, but rather to the character, wisdom, regard, and patience required to release otherwise unknown resources that will act to unravel complex realities that support and sustain rampant criminal activity. I have no idea what synergistic outcomes and strategies (like the Westside CAN center) are yet to emerge when the natural talents of all the stakeholders are unleashed in a high-trust environment of mutual respect. Please understand: *each situation is unique, and therefore solutions are unique.* You cannot take the exact solution from one area and force it upon the next. You must invest in the local community to release its own unique resources and solutions. (Citing this article on banking systems is ironic because after the success of the Westside CAN, the area got its first bank.) This presents a simple principle—when a community becomes safe and secure, economic development naturally tends to follow close behind and develops new enterprise. At the same time, economic development should not be left to chance; it should be actively pursued.

One could also consider the International Crime Free Association's efforts, whose "cornerstone of the Crime Free Programs is the partnership between law enforcement and the community working together to prevent crime." I could tell of the remarkable success that the Crime Free Program has had in the Kansas City area. The reader could go to their website and read testimonials: for example, a longtime security consultant with over a decade of experience with the Crime Free Program, who states, "I can wholeheartedly state that the Crime Free Programs ... can help even the most troubled property reclaim its dignity, profitability, and become reasonably safe."*

We will take a brief look at some other current military models, but they all tell the same stories in different ways. Putting aside all the processes and theories, the basic common denominator is *winning the hearts, minds, and trust of all the stakeholders toward a common purpose or mission.* Unfortunately, "winning the hearts and minds" is the most difficult, demanding, and laborious process any LE member or organization will ever endeavor. Here is a nonexhaustive list of reasons why winning hearts and minds is such a *demanding and unpopular* endeavor:

- It does not provide the immediate gratification (adrenaline and feelings of power) that reactionary enforcement activities provide.

* The International Crime Free Association, http://www.crime-free-association.org/testimonials.htm (accessed December 3, 2008).

- It requires so much more than the intelligence, bravery, skill, and professional persona that are required to enforce laws and effect arrests. In addition to those, it requires character, courage, patience, maturity, regard, and wisdom.
- Police lose the ready-made excuse of blaming the community for not being responsive—because "winning hearts and minds" *is* the responsibility of police.
- Everyone (from desk clerks to bureau commanders) must be accountable to have respectful regard for all persons. To accomplish this, everyone in every chain of command must courageously hold themselves and everyone else accountable—regardless of loyalties and fears. In other words, if the social system allows a commander to have a reign of terror and misery over her subordinates—*every stated value and policy to the contrary become nothing but dry ink on wasted paper.* The disregard for others will inevitably spill over into the way in which members of our communities are treated.
- It takes the job of "bean counting"—statistical analysis of work productivity—out of the realm of the simple, lazy process of counting enforcement activities in prescribed areas. This is because the focus is no longer lead measures like staffing, car checks, pedestrian checks, search warrants, and so on. Rather, the focus is on less tangible but critically important lag measures. "The test of police efficiency is the absence of crime and disorder, not the visible evidence of police action in dealing with it."[*]
- Are citizens consistently seen as people and treated with respect?
- Is the community safe, secure, and prospering—or are the "insurgents" having their way?

Emergency: Dial 911

Again, those who *choose* to spend their time reacting to what has gone wrong are doomed to spend *all their time* reacting to what has gone wrong. I return to the worn-out drumbeat of unintended consequences. Who would have thought that creating a more efficient way of summoning help and promoting its use would have unintended negative consequences? Let me say up front that I am not denying the benefits of the 911 system or advocating the demise of it. I am saying that the 911 system has likely had an unintentional consequence. It has probably accelerated what had previously been a drift in the fundamental nature of law enforcement from Noble Peace Officer to 911

[*] New Westminster Police Service website, http://www.nwpolice.org/peel.html (accessed December 13, 2008).

Reactionary Force. If we are willing to consider the possibility, only then can we consider how to repair the problem.

Let us take fire departments as an example of how *not* to settle into the routine of being reactionary. People are obviously accustomed to calling 911 for a fire, but fire departments have also proactively ensconced themselves into the fabric of modern life. Fire codes touch every building we live, work, or play in. Schoolchildren know "Stop, drop, and roll." Every person in every school actually *practices* fire alarm drills. Everyone knows that you change your smoke alarm battery biannually when you change your clocks for daylight savings time. Most building superintendents anticipate a regular visit from the fire marshal. Most electrical appliances have fire safety certifications and warnings attached. All vehicles and buildings containing materials that could be hazardous during a fire event are marked with a national marking system. I just Googled "Fire Prevention Lesson Plan" and got 389,000 results. On the first page, most of the hits for lesson plans were directed toward teachers in schools. Now ask yourself, when was the last time a child lost his life from a fire in a school?

I am not saying that police departments have neglected *all* of these proactive processes—they have engaged, particularly after September 11, 2001. But *there is a fundamental and radical difference between what it takes to be proactive with fire prevention and promoting safety and security in communities.* You see, fire prevention has the same basic properties regardless of where you are. You must separate fuel sources from ignition sources and fires from oxygen sources (firefighters, I have no expertise here, so please give me grace). Contrast that with the concept I set forth earlier: to have rampant crime or gang activity, there *must* exist ethnographic, cultural, social, historical, anthropological, and economic realities to sustain and support it. This is much more complex than fire prevention. For example, police can show you how to secure your home so that it is much more difficult to burglarize (that is a straightforward, consistent mechanical process like fire prevention). However, at some point your "fortress" begins to feel like a tomb because you live in a miserably crime-infested neighborhood (now we are talking about ethnographic, cultural, social, historical, anthropological, and economic realities).

Think of military operations. Invading a country and conquering a rogue dictator and his army make up a straightforward process—*not easy*, but comparatively simple (at least the U.S. Army made it look simple). If you can efficiently field overwhelming force, you can invade a country and defeat its military. You can do this while seeing everyone in the country as an object, devoid of personhood. The fighters are obstacles, the citizens are irrelevant, and the traitors are tools. I do not need to understand you—only crush you, push you out of my way, or manipulate you for what I want.

After the conquest, securing long-term peace and prosperity in the face of generational animosities and obstinate insurgencies is *much more complicated*. Now I must see people as people—that takes a personal anima rooted in integrity, buttressed by courage, and expressed as unconditional respect for all. Over time, these attributes enable me to develop character, patience, and wisdom. I must invest time and true compassion in order to understand individual needs, hopes, fears, and priorities. From there I must take the time to understand the ethnographic, cultural, social, historical, anthropological, and economic realities of the community. I must *listen* with humility, openness, and genuine concern. After obtaining a genuine understanding and winning the hearts and minds of all the stakeholders, I must help guide them to synergistic options that unleash their natural talents and passions.

An officer can't do this in the community if she:

- Lacks the integrity, character, and regard to have unconditional respect for all
- Is treated like an object within her own organization
- Is whizzing from call to call in a mind-numbing reactionary tizzy

The first two points are covered in this book in previous chapters, but *how do we get off the 911 hamster wheel?*

Honoring the Spirit of the Law versus the Enforcement of Laws

My own personal experience could be useful here. When I came to the academy as a twenty-one year old, I was ignorant and naïve about what I was getting into and very impressionable. While I was somewhat brave, I did not possess particularly high integrity, and I had even less courage. *However*, what I did possess was images of police work taken from the old *Adam-12* television series, which aired from about the time I was nine for roughly seven years. Now, in my late forties, I can't recall specific episodes but I can recall the "feel" and "mind-set" the episodes gave me about police work: how cops treated each other, how cops treated members of their community, how cops were responded to by members of their community, and how cops actualized police work. My academy experience did not do much to undermine my mental images—but my first "ride along" in the "hottest" zone in the city did. I had never heard so many expletives crammed into so little dialogue. All my mental images of how cops treated each other and community members were forever shattered. It was both unnerving and exhilarating to my immature heart and mind: ten hours of adrenaline four days a week—and a paycheck to boot. It was like a costume party—you get to dress up as some type of alter ego of yourself, treat people like objects, be a hero in your own mind, and have fun doing it. The only difference between this and a *real* party was that *most* of us waited until after shift to drink massive amounts of alcohol. Within a short period, I was a true convert to "law enforcement"—I "fixed" every problem by putting someone in jail. If I could not put someone in jail, I was at a loss as to why I was called to respond, much less what to do.

What's in a Name?

Could it be that the name *law enforcement* itself has contributed to a problematic mentality? Would *peace officer* or *public safety officer* be better names to reinforce the basic mission of such agencies? Granted, most agencies have community-orientated programs and processes. However, the reality hidden below the surface is much like that illustrated in the Westside CAN account of Rosa's interaction with the patrol officer. From my personal experience (some twelve years of maturing after the "costume party"), I was part of a program that had officers in middle schools teaching a life skills program. We were generally amazed at the levels of distrust and animosity we would be met with *by school administration*. It would take months or years to develop a high-trust, synergistic relationship with the school staff. I then came to dread the times when patrol officers responded to the school on calls for service. Frequently, the contemptuousness that met the school staff from patrol officers would cause a major setback in trust. Unfortunately, our "community"-orientated programs tend to be only that—programs. The officers involved in those programs are often viewed as "less than" by the rank-and-file members who actually *do* law enforcement. Much of the exponential results the Westside CAN has produced have been in *spite* of pushback—not the result of support and appreciation from the organizational rank and file. To this day, many on the KCPD see the Westside CAN as problematic to their view of the mission of law enforcement because it honors the spirit of the Law, not the mindless enforcement of individual laws. Others tell me repeatedly and with great passion that the zero-tolerance enforcement—while not effective—was the right way to honor our basic mission to enforce laws. To this day, many are angry and resentful regarding everything about the Westside CAN; they see it as deviation from the law enforcement mission and a compromise of our organizational honor.

Changing the hearts and minds of law enforcement officers is more of a challenge than one on the outside may assume at first glance. Oddly enough, I advocate a deemphasis on the *programs* of community policing. Rather, I advocate an emphasis on the basic internal *way*, anima, of each member *and the culture of organizations*. Organizations may even want to consider changing the primary name used to refer to themselves: from law enforcement back to peace officer or public safety officer. Should we consider a name change that puts the emphasis on the *goal*, peace and safety, not *one* of the *means* that we use to get to that goal, the enforcement of laws?

Understand the Link between Justice and Compassion

Others frequently make impassioned assertions that what Chip and I are advocating not only will never work but also is inherently wrong because police are a "paramilitary" organization: "We cannot coddle people and be soft because we will compromise our mission, our standards, and our safety." Little do they know the fiercest and most effective warriors in history have been those with uncompromised integrity and courage expressed in respect and compassion for others.

In reality, *justice exists only when compassion is spread abroad* and *compassion exists only when justice is spread abroad*. Let me explain this concept. Imagine you find that your ten-year-old child has been staying home "sick" from school because he is intimidated by a bully who is making his life miserable. As you talk to others, you find that this bully has a large reign of terror at the school. You also learn the school administration is aware of the problem, but their position is that they have too much compassion for all the children, *especially the bully* (given his life circumstances), to hold him accountable. I think anyone can see that what the school administrators call compassion is simply being *indulgent*; this is a *punitive counterfeit* of compassion.* This indulgence is punitive because it leaves the bully, and all his victims, suffering the emotional, psychological, and social residuals of his unaddressed problems and at the same time makes a mockery of the concept of justice. It should be easy to see that *true compassion* (empathy for others *with* a strong desire to relieve suffering), when spread abroad, sustains justice. Allow me another illustration. When I was working in middle schools (and some elementary schools) teaching a life skills program, I had the occasion to be in almost every kind of school conceivable, from deeply troubled inner-city schools, to suburban schools, to private religious schools. Even as an experienced inner-city cop, tactical officer, and detective, I had "culture shock" at the social chaos within most of the inner-city schools. At the same time, I had some of my best classes and my best times of teaching and interacting with young people at some of the most troubled schools. Ironically, I had some of my worst classes and worst times teaching at some of the better religious, suburban elementary schools. However, here was the interesting point. When I would appeal to the teachers in the most troubled schools

* C. Terry Warner, Bonds That Make Us Free: Healing Our Relationships, Coming to Ourselves (Salt Lake City, Utah: Shadow Mountain, 2001).

to support me in classroom management so that some actual learning and interaction could take place, I would often receive an incredulous look. It was as if the teachers were thinking, "How could a cop be so stupid?" Then they would say something like "Do you have any idea as to the chaotic home life of these kids? You can't expect them to come into a classroom and behave properly here when their home life is such a mess!" In contrast, I had great times of interaction and learning in friendly, fun, inviting classrooms that were also contained in the most troubled schools. I would go to the teachers, thank them profusely for their classroom management skills, and ask their secret. They would say something like "I am sure you understand the chaos of many of these young people's home life. I *must* provide them a safe, controlled classroom environment; this may be the only semblance of order they receive in life!" That is it—two radically different views of compassion. One is an indulgent punitive counterfeit that compounds suffering and hopelessness. It also, by the way, excuses and justifies lack of performance on the part of the teacher. The other represents true compassion, instills justice, and becomes the fuel of courage and regard for all. In addition, it produces superlative results. To this day, some eight years later, I get sentimental with humble admiration for these tireless, courageous teachers who pour themselves out daily into the lives of precious young people in troubling circumstances.

Reclaiming What the Military Co-opted from Police

[B]efore the counterinsurgent can win the people over,
he must take the necessary steps to really understand and know them.*

So what can we learn from the military about regard for people, compassion, and justice? In recent decades, the U.S. military has fielded the most effective fighting force the world has ever known. This force has neutralized one of the world's largest armies in short order—twice. Yet at the same time, top military brass has come to appreciate some of the most basic principles historically related to old-fashioned policing. In early 2007 General Petraeus, himself holding a PhD in international studies from Princeton University, assembled a team of other "warrior scholars": a unique team of individuals with combat experience in Iraq and academic doctorates. The assembled team was to hone Petraeus's vision of counterinsurgency (COIN) for Iraq. The process requires a significant understanding of local culture and

* Lieutenant Colonel Jack Marr, U.S. Army; Major John Cushing, U.S. Army; Major Brandon Garner, U.S. Army; and Captain Richard Thompson, U.S. Army, "Human Terrain Mapping: A Critical First Step to Winning the COIN Fight," Military Review, March–April 2008.

demographics, so the "warrior scholar" team fit the bill.* What has resulted is the philosophy represented in documents such as the September 16, 2008, issue of the *Headquarters, Multinational Force Iraq's Counterinsurgency Guidance* publication, which states under the subtitle "How We Think,"

> The environment in which we operate is complex and demands that we employ every weapon in our arsenal, both kinetic and non-kinetic. To fully utilize all approaches we must understand the local culture and history. Learn about the tribes, formal and informal leaders … understand how the society functions.[†]

How what the military has discovered relates to the basic mission of public safety organizations is so blatantly obvious that it seems redundant for me to comment. Police organizations in the United States have many weapons in their arsenal, and the most effective ones are *nonkinetic*. In order to utilize all resources, one must understand the local culture and issues. In order to understand, one must listen. In order to listen, one must have unconditional respect for all. In order to have unconditional respect for all, one must have an internal anima rooted in integrity and buttressed by courage. To remind ourselves of the link to Robert Peel's principles:

- The ability of the police to perform their duties is dependent upon public approval of police actions.
- Police must secure the willing cooperation of the public in voluntary observance of the law to be able to secure and maintain the respect of the public.
- The degree of cooperation of the public that can be secured diminishes proportionately to the necessity of the use of physical force.[‡]

In the article cited from the *Military Review*, the authors observe that the original COIN operations in Iraq and Afghanistan were not prepared for the realities that faced them. It did not take long for studies of success to demonstrate the following: "Overwhelmingly, the units that seemed to be winning the fight had made significant inroads with local leaders, had found proactive ways to understand and respect local cultural norms, and had addressed specific community needs."[§] The military writers go on to make this critical observation that speaks to the basic mission of police agencies. They note that by understanding and addressing people's priority needs, they

---

* James Joyner, "Petraeus' Princeton PhD Posse," Outside the Belt Way, February 5, 2007, http://www.outsidethebeltway.com/archives/petraeus_princeton_phd_posse_/ (accessed December 13, 2008).
† http://www.mnf-iraq.com/images/CGs_Messages/odierno_coin_guidance.pdf (accessed September 5, 2009).
‡ New Westminster Police Service website, http://www.nwpolice.org/peel.html (accessed December 13, 2008).
§ Marr, Cushing, Garner, and Thompson, "Human Terrain Mapping."

could cultivate relationships and build trust with neighborhood leaders.* If the references from this military article sound familiar, think of the Westside CAN story. The cited article has much to say about the processes the military uses that may be useful to policing, but for our purposes, there is one central point. The most overwhelming, shocking, and devastating manmade force the world has ever known—the current U.S. military—has discovered and utilized one of the most basic and historic "soft skills" of policing.

Again, I know the next argument: "So what—the 'new Army' top brass has hired some soft social workers to screw things up." First, the concept of unconditional respect producing fantastic mission advancement is not new to the military. Major Sherwood Moran, who served in the Pacific theater of World War II and sets the Marine "gold standard" in interrogation of enemy prisoners of war, had this to say:

> "You can get a 'confession' out of a man by bullying him, by practicing 'third degree' methods—but an intelligence officer is not interested in confessions," he said. "He is after information, and it has been demonstrated time and again that a human approach works best."†

As could be expected, field-grade officers frequently criticized Moran as being "soft," and some advocated simply shooting the prisoners. The same officers later found themselves begging for solid information that could come only from captured prisoners. With this mission, Moran's respectful way of behaving toward prisoners proved to be the gold standard for gathering critical information that saved countless lives.‡

The second problem with the "soft social worker" pushback is the Phase IV culmination exercise of Special Forces Training, which includes a nineteen-day field training exercise called "Robin Sage." "This exercise involves the students, counterinsurgent and guerrilla personnel (other service members), auxiliary personnel, and cadre. This scenario stresses realism because the student SFODAs (special forces operational detachment alpha) must train a mock guerilla force in a hostile environment using civilians in the surrounding community as the auxiliary."§ This essentially amounts to *winning the hearts, minds, and trust of all the stakeholders toward a common purpose or mission.*

So, to my friends in law enforcement who wish to label the *tough-as-nails* men who volunteer, qualify, and make it through U.S. Army Special

---

* Ibid.
† Lieutenant Colonel James B. Wilkinson, USMC (Ret.), with Dick Camp, "The Gold Standard Major Sherwood Moran and the Interrogation of Prisoners of War," The Spot Report (Journal of the Marine Corps Interrogator Translator Teams Association) 5, no. 2 (Winter 2007–2008), MCITTA (Marine Corps Interrogator Translator Teams Association).
‡ Wilkinson, "The Gold Standard."
§ First Special Warfare Training Group (Airborne), http://www.globalsecurity.org/military/agency/army/1swtg.htm (accessed December 21, 2008).

Forces training as "soft social workers," please do so in the privacy of your own mind. Moreover, to those who push against what we advocate because law enforcement is "paramilitary," I say, "A-men, let's become *more* like the military!"

Conclusion

Getting off the "911 hamster wheel" begins with the following: (1) there must be a fundamental change in the hearts and minds of law enforcement members, that is, the development of personal anima; (2) all citizens must be seen and treated as people, with genuine respect; (3) community policing must no longer be primarily program based, and building partnership must become a fundamental mind-set and mission of all members; (4) true understanding of underlying causal realities must be gained through active and empathic listening with genuine compassion; and (5) accountability processes must shift from lead measures such as staffing and enforcement activities to the four factors just listed and the basic presuppositions enumerated at the beginning of this chapter.

Now the big question: how? Chapter 9 will present an overview of the process only just initiated on the KCPD to begin to "*anima*te" the culture.

Unconditional Respect
The Building of Character

8

A man's character is his fate.

—**Heraclitus**

I had briefed my squad thoroughly on what to expect on this particular raid. The suspects had been known to be armed with firearms, and to have ties to a local gang who deeply resented the police. We were going to the house just before 11:00 p.m. to serve a high-risk search warrant, which was the culminating affair in a two-month investigation of rampant drug sales in and around the residence. As I made the turn on the target street, my team was poised in the back of the van, weapons at the ready, muscles tense. A quiet calm descended as these professionals made last-minute mental preparations. The unmistakable sense of anticipation—a feeling I had felt a thousand times before while among these very men—hung in the air. I knew they were ready for whatever threat waited on the other side of the door, which was about to come crashing down under the weight of a sixty-pound ram, currently being lofted by one of my strongest operators.

The vehicle doors came open as I eased the van to a stop at the curb just north of the house. The men piled out silently as I put the van in park and made my way toward the curb to join my team. The approach was silent and skillful; I couldn't help but think of how countless hours of training paid huge dividends in the real world. When the team reached the porch, I observed an unknown male peer out of a dirty, cracked window that faced the street. Upon seeing what he had to know was inevitable, he turned and ran deeper into the structure. He was carrying something in his right hand.

The point man announced, "Police, we have a search warrant!" as the breacher hit the door with such force the wood frame splintered, knocking the door off the hinges and sending the deadbolt sailing into what served as the dining room. The point man crossed the threshold and hooked tight to his left, as the two-man (the second man through the door whose primary job is to cover the point man) trained his rifle on the suspect who had run toward a bedroom located off the dining area. The suspect was in full autonomic nervous system activation, his mind racing in "fight-or-flight" mode. He wisely chose the latter and dumped what he was carrying—a sawed-off .12 gauge shotgun with the serial number ground off—on the floor of what was later determined to be a child's bedroom, as two red laser dots played across his forehead. I respected this man's humanity. He was not just a "crack head" who would continue to flee in a rush of panic, but a man with thoughts and feelings who was very capable of reacting with extreme violence and unpredictability. He was an opponent who needed to be respected for his ability to do harm.

The suspect—along with an adult female and six small children—were detained inside the residence. Once the initial protective sweep was completed, the point man shouted, "All clear!" The phrase was echoed from man to man until I acknowledged it, signifying the house was now safe for us to occupy. I removed my helmet and mask to address the occupants of the home, who had been escorted to the living room. The adrenaline in my system had subsided, and I was immediately introduced to the pungent odor of animal feces emanating throughout the house. I noticed the temperature inside was no warmer than it had been when I was standing on the front porch in the cold February air. My breath steamed out in puffs of odorless smoke, signifying near-freezing conditions inside the house. I reiterated who we were to the two adults and checked to ensure that neither they nor the children had been injured during our initial entry into the home. I answered a couple of quick questions concerning the scope of the search warrant, and then set about walking through the house to take a closer look around. My job has taken me into some of the nastiest places anyone would want to visit, but the condition of this particular residence flirted with the idea of shocking what little sensibilities to filth I had left. The house had no electricity, no heat, no gas, and no running water. There were several windows broken out, which allowed the wintry air to saturate the structure. I found human waste in the bathtub, and about a year's worth of dog feces on the floor of the basement. The smell of ammonia floated in the air so strongly that my eyes watered. The only working appliance was a television that was being powered by an extension cord that ran from the house next door. The residence was littered with food scraps, which the roaches readily feasted on, and amongst it all sat the children, ages three months to six years old. They were piled under dirty blankets on a grimy couch in the corner of the front room. Their faces showed terror at the presence of these hulking strangers who carried guns and spoke in serious, hushed tones. One of my men located a bag of crack cocaine in a child's room, which had long ago been abandoned to the rodents. Another bag of drugs was lying on the floor by the end table near the couch. My empathy for the children was beginning to be overcome by a rising tide of anger. I was battling a strong desire to drag the man and woman out of the house by their throats. In mere seconds, I saw the lives of these kids flash through my mind. I felt their hopelessness. I saw unexamined lives with little chance at the realization of purposefulness. I could sense the same wave of emotions coming from my team—all fathers and extremely attentive family men. The collective emotion rising from my team seemed to embrace the potential to ignite the house around us. Somebody just had to pay for the injustice visited upon these poor young children.

I have spent countless hours upon hours honing my physical and mental capabilities to prepare me to deal with the high-stress nature of my chosen profession. Physically, I must be strong to carry my equipment and control people who insist on fighting or resisting arrest. Mentally, my mind must be clear and open to interpretation of environmental stimuli that alert me to danger. I must be sensitive to subtleties that would have little meaning to a layman, or someone blinded by his own arrogance, but can be indispensable to the safety of the team. I also must rely on my anima to guide me to act for what is right, and not be blinded by my natural tendency to be judgmental.

We don't hear law enforcement officers talk much about the development of character, but I would declare it is even more critical than mental and physical maturity when dealing with people. The way an officer treats people—especially people he cannot seem to relate to—is a direct reflection of his character, and while some may use it as a justification for mistreatment, in reality it has little to do with the behavior of those he comes in contact with during the course of his duties. By focusing our energies on developing a sturdy anima—or inner armor—we are ultimately able to influence others more effectively. This anima represents our true internal way. It is rooted in integrity, buttressed by courage, and expressed as unconditional respect for all people.

Integrity

Integrity is acting for what is right regardless of our personal biases, fears, prejudices, and loyalties. It requires strict discipline and the dedication to build systems of accountability that will ensure appropriate discernment in the most difficult of circumstances. A person with integrity displays a consistency of action that is married to deeply held principles of right and wrong.

Leadership guru and author Gus Lee says that integrity has three parts:

- Discern right from wrong
- Act for what is right regardless of risk to self
- Teach others from that act of integrity*

How often do you suppose we *automatically* discern right from wrong regardless of our personal biases, fears, prejudices, and loyalties? We agree that the answer is almost never. In fact, we need our personal biases, fears,

* Gus Lee, Courage: The Backbone of Leadership (San Francisco: Jossey-Bass, 2006).

prejudices, and loyalties to navigate our way in the world. Without them, we would be like naïve two year olds stumbling through life aimlessly, constantly at the mercy of things that we do not understand and that are beyond our control.

My cousin Chad and his wife, Heather, are blessed with one of the most beautiful families anyone could ask for. Their Colorado home has a fireplace with a glass enclosure in the den. When the fireplace is on, the heat from the flames warms the glass to a scalding temperature. When their children were toddlers, Chad and Heather were always careful to keep them far away from the fireplace for fear they would get burned. As you can imagine, the fireplace seemed very warm and inviting to a young child who had no experience with the dangers of fire. One day, Chad shut down the fireplace and let it cool before opening up the den to the children. It had been off for approximately 45 minutes, which seemed like more than enough time to allow the glass to cool sufficiently. His youngest daughter, Kate, who was 14 months old at the time, ambled into the den. She walked along the wall and—before anyone could react—placed her hands on the glass that covered the front of the fireplace. The glass had not cooled off completely, and Kate's little hands were seared on the hot surface. Following this incident, Chad and Heather did not have to worry about Kate ever getting close to the fireplace again. She didn't even want to be in the same room with it. You see, she had developed a very necessary bias against the fireplace—one that would prevent her from suffering a similar injury in the future.

We all are limited in our view of the world. We each see a different world because of our subjective perceptions. It is very necessary to have personal fears, biases, prejudices, and loyalties. They allow us to make calculated decisions in an unpredictable world. One certainly could not be a police officer without them. The essence of integrity, then, is to be able to discern right from wrong not because we have eliminated these internal filters, but *in spite of* our natural tendency to project our subjective values onto the world around us.

Consider the natural ability that we as humans have to justify our behaviors. The word *justify* is used in the construction trade to mean "to make straight." When a structure is being erected and a wall is crooked, the builders must justify it to make it straight. We pervert our fears, biases, prejudices, and loyalties to serve as justifications for crooked behavior when we fail to act for what is right. Whenever I find myself justifying a behavior I am engaged in, the first thing it does is awaken me to knowledge that the behavior is probably crooked. Remember—behavior that is straight doesn't need justification. Imagine you are walking into a convenience store to grab a cup of coffee between calls for service, and you see an elderly lady spill her purse. You stop to help her pick up the contents and hand them back to her. Would you then turn to your partner and "justify" or explain why you helped the lady? Probably not; straight behavior does not need to be justified.

An anima rooted in integrity helps us recognize when our internal safety mechanisms start to act as self-justifications for crooked behavior. It permits us to look at ourselves critically and examine our commitment to act for what is right, and allows us to compensate for our natural tendency to be self-deceived. Integrity serves as the foundation on which to build an anima capable of helping us navigate the sea of self-interest that clouds our ability to judge right from wrong.

Courage

Integrity allows us to know the right thing, but it is courage that strengthens our ability to act for what is right. An anima that is buttressed by courage ensures we have the fortitude to push forward regardless of the social pressures that act to discourage us. In Chapter 1, we introduced the concept that bravery represents physical strength and courage represents moral strength and commitment. Bravery is often used synonymously with courage, but they are not the same. We feel not only that this distinction is important in police work but also that it is critical to draw this distinction. For example, an officer running into a gun battle to help others without wearing a bullet-resistant vest is a demonstration of bravery. A fellow officer later pulling that same officer aside and having a candid conversation with her about her decision not to wear a vest on duty is an example of courage. To reiterate what we stated in the opening chapter, bravery can be thought of as acting for what is right when one's social grouping agrees with the act. It requires courage to act for what is right when one's social grouping *does not* agree with the act. Our culture is quick to award bravery, but most often, our social systems and structural policies work to *dis*courage our officers from standing on principle. I have actually spoken to many officers who insist they would not stand up to a supervisor making poor decisions even if those decisions placed them and others in physical danger. Their reasoning is that the social climate simply doesn't support questioning the chain of command. They say we have a rank structure for a reason and it is not their place to question the decisions of those above them. What they are really saying is they *don't care enough* to act for what is right when the social environment does not support the act. (See the Rule of 30 in Chapter 2.) The same officers who would willingly take a bullet for a comrade shy away from having a difficult conversation with a coworker, even when that same coworker is engaged in behavior that places their very career and livelihood at risk.

I was teaching a raid-planning class in another state last year. About two hours into the class, a young SWAT sergeant in the back of the room raised his hand. He said, "Chip, I have a question. I have asked this question everywhere I go, and I have never been able to get a straight answer. You seem like a pretty smart guy [that was his first mistake], and I want to run it by you." He had definitely put me on the spot, and I told him I would do my best to answer his question. He proceeded to tell me that he worked for a SWAT commander whose decisions did not seem to be in the best interest of the safety of the team. When I asked him to explain, he said he had been to a lot of SWAT training and many instructors like me had stood in the front of the class talking about protocol for dealing with subjects who are armed and barricaded and do not have hostages. He said all the instructors agreed that the safest tactic was to draw the subject out of the structure and bring him to the team, versus going in after him. He went on to elaborate several methods he had learned for coaxing a subject out of a barricaded situation, including the use of tear gas to make the environment undesirable. He related that his SWAT commander did not believe in "tearing up people's houses." Each time they had a subject who was barricaded in a house and thought to be armed, the commander would forgo any attempt to gas the house and order him to lead his team into the structure to go and get the subject. He related, "I always protest and tell my commander it isn't safe and someone could get hurt, but he gives me an order to go in and I have no choice but to lead my team in. My question is: What is the problem with my commander?" I told him I didn't have the slightest idea. He looked dejected and threw up his hands. He said he was disappointed because he thought I would be the one person who would finally tell him what the problem was. I replied, "Oh…. I don't know what is wrong with your commander, but I know what the problem is." He seemed elated and once again asked what the problem was. I replied, "You're the problem. The problem is you're afraid." The blood drained out of his face, and he became defensive. He told me he had been commended for his bravery on numerous occasions. I told him I wasn't questioning his bravery—I was questioning his courage. He seemed confused, so I asked him, "What did you do before you became a SWAT supervisor?" He told me he had been a road deputy. I asked him if he would like to go back to being a road deputy, and he said, "No way." I stated, "I know that, and your commander knows that too. You have trained him that all he has to do is put up with a little pushback from you when he tells you to do something unsafe, then he will give you an order and you will go ahead and do it anyway. You have sent him a clear message that you will not act for what is right because you care more about your assignment as a SWAT supervisor than about the safety of your men. The insidious thing is that you have sent your men the same message. When you have the courage to put the safety of your men above your own careerism, then you will refuse to endanger them and the problem will cease to exist."

He pulled me aside on the next break and asked, "What you said in the class … that's the answer, isn't it?" I told him I thought it was. He asked me, "What is going to happen the first time I tell my commander

I am not taking my men into an unsafe situation just because it is convenient?" I replied, "He is going to fire your ass and put someone in your place that will do what he is told. But that isn't the point. The point is that you will send him another type of message. You will let him know he was in the presence of a man with character. You will also demonstrate to your men that you care more about their lives than about your own self-interest." I ended by telling him that, more often than not, no one is going to throw you a parade or pin a medal on your chest for standing on principle. It is more likely that you will be shunned and sometimes face negative consequences. The pursuit of high core values is not for the weak of spirit. Acting for what is right has got to be its own reward. I have still not heard back from the gentlemen, but I sincerely hope he was able to find the courage to act for what he knew in his heart was the right thing.

The Foundations of Character

> Courage isn't simply one of the virtues; it's the form of every virtue at the point of testing.
>
> —C. S. Lewis

Throughout this book, we have advocated a consistent "inner way," or anima. Popular leadership and self-help doctrine tend to focus on behaviors as a way of achieving what you want or controlling outcomes. They tell us that we must discipline ourselves to behave in certain ways to influence others. This type of thinking focuses on action. On the surface, it seems logical and straightforward; however, action in and of itself is meaningless without the relevant context. Action does, therefore, derive its significance from the context in which it is presented.

Anima is the inner essence of what we are to the world. It refers to our internal way, as opposed to the image we may attempt to present to the people with whom we interact. It says that what we do—or the action we take—is not nearly as relevant as how we are inside when we act. This is an incredibly important distinction. The difference between what we are and what we do defines our destiny. The internal anima that we advocate exists for intentionally aligning our internal selves, what we are, with our external behaviors, what we do. To do otherwise, to pretend I can behave one way (disdainful of others) while maintaining high character, is self-deceptive. This is like the well-used analogy of CO gas poisoning. It is deadly to self and others, *because* it is cloaked and insidious. When these two aspects of our being (inner and behavior) are properly aligned, we possess a power of effectiveness and influence that is experienced only by those of the highest character.

I will illustrate the relevance of character using a metaphor. Consider a newly constructed home. The foundation is the first part of any building or home that is completed. How important is the foundation? I mean, what if the workers hurried to complete it and skipped several steps? What if they were in such a rush to get the home built that they didn't allow the foundation the proper amount of time to set? I surmise it wouldn't matter how hard the framers worked or how masterfully the rest of the home was constructed. Without a solid foundation, the home would eventually come crashing down around the occupants. The foundation is a critically important part of the construction process. It takes time, patience, and the proper tools to ensure it is solid and able to support the weight of the structure during the most unforgiving of weather. The proper anima (raw materials, craftsmanship) is vital to the construction of a solid character (foundation).

Character is a core competency that is forever in the making. The development of character is a lifelong pursuit. We are faced with daily challenges and opportunities to strengthen or weaken our character. Our character is strengthened when we integrate our inner way with our outward behaviors. It is weakened when we fail to act in a manner consistent with what is right—when we fail to "walk our talk." Gus Lee says, "Character is the result of sustained integrity and courage.... [C]haracter is the most challenging core value because it requires a lifetime to fulfill."*

What characteristics are common to someone with a highly developed anima? Unconditional respect is the physical manifestation of our developed inner way. It is what our anima "looks" like to the rest of the world. Remember, how we see and treat others is a direct reflection of our character. It has to do with us responding appropriately to the person and situation and should have nothing to do with our personal judgments of their character or lifestyle.

Consider for a moment physical strength. How important is the development of physical strength in helping a police officer to be conditioned and skilled? How important is this type of potency when an officer must control a drug-crazed suspect or push a stalled car out of the roadway? It is incredibly important. Now, how do we develop our physical strength? There are a variety of proven methods. You can use everything from free-weight training to calisthenics to Pilates, yoga, or universal weight machines. All of these methods rely on the same principle to develop the muscles—repetition and resistance. It takes resistance and repetition to build physical strength, and the more resistance we employ over time, the stronger we are able to become. If we choose to avoid resistance training, we may be able to carry on for a while, but in the long run, when we betray our bodies by neglecting physical conditioning, our

* Lee, Courage.

bodies will expose our lack of commitment and we will break down at the times we—or others who depend on us—need our strength the most. We will be more injury prone and more susceptible to all sorts of illness and stress-related conditions. We will become weak and unable to protect our fellow citizens. I am talking about the development of personal strength and skills needed to be properly trained, conditioned, and prepared. The often employed alternative is to attempt to "appear" tough and capable by employing disdainful attitudes and abusive behaviors. It is all too simple to try to appear tough; however, developing the kind of skill necessary to be truly capable of handling the most dangerous of circumstances takes hard work, discipline, and a personal commitment to overcome our tendency to be self-deceived.

Now, apply the concept of resistance and repetition to the development of a strong character. Just as our bodies require resistance and repetition to get stronger, so does our character. The principle of resistance training for our bodies revolves around the way the muscles are broken down only to grow back stronger, more defined, and capable of handling increasing workloads. This same principle is at work with character building. While physical resistance can be artificially created (consider the use of weights in the gym), the kind of resistance needed for character development can be only indirectly created. On the other hand, difficult people and challenging situations constantly provide that resistance.

With so much time spent trying to *avoid* conflict, it is no wonder that we are experiencing a crisis of character in our society. We are taught that it is better to not stand too tall for what is right because we may offend someone and invite conflict. What results is a pattern of conflict avoidance, or resistance avoidance, that atrophies our character so that it becomes soft and frail. The irony is that without conflict (which we intentionally avoid), we have no way of strengthening our characters to deal with difficult circumstances. Noted educator Helen Keller said, "Character cannot be developed in ease and quiet. Only through experience of trial and suffering can the soul be strengthened, ambition inspired, and success achieved."*

When we interact with challenging people while possessing an attitude of unconditional respect, our character becomes stronger and more resilient. The first step in the development of character is to not allow ourselves the convenient self-deception of seeing others as "less than" us and as objects so that we are excused from acting for what is right. This allows me to see and act with integrity. From that point, compassion and justice will likely lead me to confront difficult circumstances. Like I mentioned, with physical training, we can create "artificial" resistance to prepare our bodies for conflict, but this is generally not so when it comes to resistance that builds our

---

* Helen Keller, The Story of My Life (1903; reprint, New York: Signet, 1988).

character. There are very few ways* to artificially simulate character-building challenges. Fortunately, these types of situations exist all around us: with our families, friends, coworkers, and clientele. All that is needed is for us to exercise and build courage to take advantage of these opportunities when they arise.

Character and Leadership

British Field Marshal Bernard Montgomery, who played an important role in the Allied victories in North Africa and Europe during World War II, said, "Leadership is the capacity and will to rally men and women to a common purpose and the character which inspires confidence." Without character there can be no true leadership, regardless of whether you are leading a SWAT team on a search warrant, organizing a block watch program, or working with a civil affairs unit to rebuild a school in Iraq. A leader with character possesses the power to inspire others to be their best selves and achieve more collectively than they ever could as individuals. This type of leader possesses a developed anima and will act for what is right, regardless of the risk to self and regardless of what his or her social grouping thinks of the act. When a leader chooses to act for what is right, she must be content in the knowledge that it will probably not bring her accolades or recognition. Much of the time, acting with integrity makes one the focus of controversy and disdain. Acting for what is right *must* be its own reward.

I have had the pleasure of knowing many leaders with true character. One such leader is Jerry West. A few years back, Jerry was the sergeant and team leader of a SWAT team for the Missouri State Highway Patrol (MSHP). Jerry acted with integrity and "walked the talk" on a daily basis. He was well respected within the team and the entire agency. Jerry faced a crisis of conscious when he repeatedly requested proper training and equipment for his team, but was denied these crucial assets by his superiors. He was faced with a choice. He could either allow his team to be put at risk and thus protect his position, or take a stand for his men by confronting the reality of the situation. Jerry approached his commander and expressed his concerns a final time. When the needs of the team weren't met, Jerry resigned his position as team leader and left the SWAT team. Jerry was so respected by his team that most of

---

* One key example is practicing a courageous communication model in role-play scenarios. By practicing the skill set, it acts as stress inoculation training and increases skill. This makes one more likely to step up and have a difficult conversation in real-world applications (which takes courage). This is the building of character, indirectly caused by practicing the skill in an artificially created environment. This is different but analogous to physical training. We do not typically develop physical strength for the weight room; we do so for real-life application of the strength gained in the gym.

the men resigned their positions in the team. The team had to be rebuilt from the ground up, and Jerry's sacrifice became known throughout the agency, reaffirming what others already knew—that Jerry was a man of character.

I had the opportunity to discuss this event with Jerry recently. I recognized the fact that he had to give up a position that he loved because of principle, and that his situation was an example of how acting for what is right must be its own reward. Jerry was quick to correct me. He said, "Chip, I may have lost a job I loved, but the SWAT team members who replaced me and my men are provided with all the training and equipment they need to do their jobs safely, and that is very rewarding." Jerry was promoted sometime later and now serves as a lieutenant with the state patrol. He is currently the assistant director of the MSHP Law Enforcement Academy, where his character is on display for each new recruit who walks through the doors.

While a person's observable behavior is an indication of character, a truly developed character is the result of a deep internal way (anima) that is rooted in integrity and buttressed by courage.

Animating a Culture   9

Ever more people today have the means to live, but no meaning to live for.

—**Viktor E. Frankl**[*]

As a presupposition of this book, the anima (inner way) we have been advocating *is* a positive social contagion. It can and will transform a police (or any, for that matter) organizational culture and the community (or customer base) it serves.

This chapter will include a comprehensive road map to "*animate*" any culture. Please note the nuance here. A road map lays out a process for arriving at a destination; it does not fill in all the details (where you stop for fuel, food, recreation, rest, etc.). These details will be unique to each circumstance. The *animating* process takes into consideration the reality pressing upon us mentioned in the first chapter of this book: *It takes only a cursory reading of history, or the daily newspaper, to conclude that humans hold a unique status. They can be the most dangerous, selfish, cruel, and unpredictable—and the most trustworthy, altruistic, kind, and dependable—of creatures. Even more perplexing is that the same individual will occasionally make headlines as being polar opposites from the perspective of their victims versus that of their family and friends.* This chapter also takes into consideration this stance as recorded in *APA Online*, the American Psychological Association's online journal, by an expert witness in the Abu Ghraib prison scandal (as also discussed in the first chapter):

> That line between good and evil is permeable…. Any of us can move across it…. I argue that we all have the capacity for love and evil—to be Mother Theresa, to be Hitler or Saddam Hussein. It's the situation that brings that out.[†]

The application of these realities calls for comprehensive systems that create a "situation" that *brings out* the "Mother Theresa" and not the "Hitler or Saddam Hussein" in individuals (so to speak). It may be helpful to think of the need for comprehensive environmental systems with an illustration using

---

[*] Brainy Quote, http://www.brainyquote.com/quotes/quotes/a/aldoushuxl101185.html (accessed November 13, 2008).

[†] Melissa Dittman, "What Makes Good People Do Bad Things?" APA Online: Monitor on Psychology 35, no. 9 (October 2004): http://www.apa.org/monitor/oct04/goodbad.html. In this article, former APA president Philip Zimbardo drew from research to help explain evil under the backdrop of recent Iraqi prisoner abuses at Abu Ghraib.

the current concern over the H1N1 flu (swine flu). It seems as though the primary concern (spring of 2009) with the H1N1 is that there is no immunization. Like other flu viruses, it apparently spreads from infected persons to others through coughing, sneezing, and contact with contaminated surfaces. Obviously if people are sick, they are expected to limit their contact with others, and use proper etiquette when coughing or sneezing.

The problem of "situations" bringing out good or evil is that *most* situations *naturally* tend to perpetuate a low level of simmering evil thoughts and behaviors. Consider this illustration to explain why: let's say that each of us is "contaminated" with a "social virus" called the *S1OO flu* (where *S1OO* stands for "Self #1—Others Objects"). When we have contact with others, the virus becomes exponentially virulent because the OO portion in one carrier brews up hybrids in the S1 portion in the other infected person, and vice versa. Since we are always all "infected," simply avoiding contact with others is impossible. Even when we are not in direct contact with others, everything in our culture feeds our "virus." Media advertising bombards us constantly with self-centeredness-feeding messages and expectations. Even casual contact, such as passing by others, can provoke this virus with thoughts and feelings of envy and entitlement as we subconsciously and relentlessly compare such things as status, physical appearance, clothing, jewelry, vehicles, and companionship. Just as it is currently with the swine flu, for the S1OO flu there never will be an immunization or any antiviral treatments. The only resource to combat it is what we might call the *AIOE contra flu* (where *AIOE* stands for "Anima, rooted in Integrity that sees Others as people who are Equally important to us"). This contra flu will combat the insidious personal and social decaying realities of the S1OO flu. When the S1OO flu runs unchecked, integrity evaporates in a "might makes right" torrent. Others are objects to be manipulated to get what I want, get out of my way, or get ignored by the almighty Self. It is automatic and natural for others who are being seen and treated as objects, and also infected with S1 (Self #1), to respond in the following ways:

- Blindly and mindlessly accepting the terms of conflict (might makes right) by the power holder. This becomes a *psychological contract* through which we interpret all other events.
- Abandoning enduring principles of right and wrong.
- Using subversive aggression directed at the organization and community that seeps into communal attitudes, lives, and dialogue. This becomes a *social contract* through which expectations are formed and groupthink solidifies.*

---

* For a discussion on how these contracts form in organizations, see Denise M. Rousseau, Psychological Contracts in Organizations Understanding Written and Unwritten Agreements (Thousand Oaks, Calif.: Sage, 1995).

I see this frequently when dealing with those afflicted by unfairness in an organization. They hate the objectified (i.e., reduced to object status) treatment, but at the same time buy in by objectifying others (in a 360° outflow): "I hate the way you see and treat me as an object, but I accept your terms of engagement, and will reciprocate by seeing and treating you and everyone else as an object. Because I can't rely on *your* character, I can't rely on *mine* either. Because you use direct and subversive manipulation tactics against me, I will use the same on you. I *say* I hate it, but the virus is *in* me. I am mindlessly drawn into others corruption and treachery—like a moth to a consuming flame. The rules of this heinous game are somehow woven into my psyche at the most fundamental level; I play by its nefarious regulations by blind, mindless default."

If organizational leaders do nothing, that is exactly what they will get, reciprocating hostilities and cynicism. This is the prevailing social environment for many law enforcement agencies; unfortunately, they have become so accustomed to it they don't question it anymore. I recently sat dumbfounded in a meeting with people I wrongly assumed would welcome deep organizational change because they had felt victimized by the status quo (S1OO) for so long. Some of the Leadership Academy initiatives (resetting the social context by using AIOE) had given them a voice of influence at the table. But they came to the table with all the blinding presuppositions of the old rule book (S1OO). I quickly bowed out, knowing I had come ill prepared because of my assumptions and had consequently failed to set the context for the meeting around AIOE. The unstated agenda was "Might makes right, and now we have some might to make our own right with." The only prospect to combat the natural insidious spread of the S1OO flu is that every environmental structure in an organization and community must support and propagate the AIOE contra flu as a positive social contagion.

I don't want to make this sound hopeless, but it will be challenging to transform a culture with a long-standing tradition, history, and engrained social contracts. Even the most base and dysfunctional of internal and social attitudes and presuppositions can become ingrained into the fabric of an organization and seem normative regardless of how destructive they are. To explain this by revisiting the previous illustration of carbon monoxide poisoning from Chapter 1, the *sufferer automatically tends to blame something else for any symptoms regardless of the intensity of evidence to the contrary.* A newly promoted sergeant recently told me of when he and his wife purchased a "fixer-upper" home. Fortunately, his father-in-law had encouraged him to purchase a carbon monoxide detector. The day he plugged in the CO detector, it started to give a warning. He assumed that it was malfunctioning and began trying to figure out what the problem was. While trying to figure this out, he noticed that he and his wife were each feeling sick and getting progressively worse. He continued to attempt to figure out what was wrong with his brand-new CO detector when he noticed the goldfish was dead. He continued on his quest to "fix" the broken CO detector. When the new detector would not quit giving a warning regardless of how many times he reset it, he finally relented and called the Fire Department. He later found that his house did indeed have lethal levels of CO. Imagine the tragedy of parents (with no CO detector) in a house filling with the deadly but odorless gas. Seeing themselves and their beloved children become increasingly ill, they assume that "we all got food poisoning" and decide to "sleep it off" in the same environment that is killing them.* If the parents could, *for even a moment*, entertain a thought such as "What if there is a flaw in *my* presuppositions about what the problem *really* is?" or, to go back to the previous flu virus illustration, what if one could think, "The deadly S1OO virus is in *me!*" If that were the case, all kinds of possible understandings and solutions would open up to them. But alas, we are not hardwired in that manner. We automatically tend to assume the following:

- The way I see something is the way it is.
- The way I feel about someone is the way he or she is.
- The way I remember an event is the way it was.
- If you disagree with me, you are stupid, a liar, or psychotic (disconnected from reality).

The irony is that this assumptive thought base (all problems and misunderstandings are external to me) IS the apex of *self-imposed* ignorance, deception, and even psychosis. Probably the only reason it is not considered pathological is that it is endemic. So—don't think this comes easy for your organization or the KCPD. As you read this, keep in mind that some of this has been institutionalized in the KCPD through Leadership Academy and various initiatives. Some of this is in process; some has yet to be initiated.

I do not know who to attribute this quote to; I have heard it so much from many sources, none of whom claims authorship, and I am at a loss. However, it is extremely relevant at this point: "Healthy people talk to themselves; unhealthy people listen to themselves." For our context, what we naturally hear if we listen to ourselves is the voice of the S1OO virus. What we *must force* into our conscience is the AIOE virus way of thinking. At this point, the S1OO virus would say something like the following: "Since I am not the chief executive officer or the chief of police and since the culture is so pervasively entrenched, there is nothing I can do and therefore I will *not even try*. It is literal career suicide to stand for what is right with courageous, genuine, respectful conversation and actions." This is the main pushback I have received from all but a stalwart few over the last several years, both inside and outside of law enforcement. Aldous

---

* Sadly and ironically, as I was writing this chapter and after writing this imaginary story, my wife told me of a real family of four having been found dead of carbon monoxide poisoning. They had won a fundraising auction to get to stay in a brand-new $9 million cabin in Aspen, Colorado. See http://abcnews.go.com/US/story?id=6376209&page=1 (accessed December 4, 2009).

Huxley captured the brutal truth: "Cynical realism is the intelligent man's best excuse for doing nothing in an intolerable situation."* On the contrary; for all intents and purposes, the process I am writing about in this chapter, although by no means complete (in fact, barely off to a good solid start) for the Kansas City Police Department, began when an *officer* (bottom of the rank structure) was loaned the book *Courage: The Backbone of Leadership* by Gus and Diane Lee. I was challenged with my own lack of personal integrity, courage, and character. I was also struck by the glaring application of high core values and the unconditional respect that flows from them upon law enforcement. I simply began by writing an article on unconditional respect (having it vetted) and circulating the article and teaching the concept whenever possible. What initially fascinated me was the level of animosity and pushback I received from many department members. The process has greatly evolved, with even Gus Lee himself graciously supporting the efforts, and helping me overcome my own ignorance about how a culture is inspired. It has become a rather complex mixture of initiatives. Many department members have become ardent supporters (primarily, but by *no means limited to*, my Leadership Academy collaborator Officer Daniel Schmer, Sergeant Douglas "Skip" Cox, Captain James Thomas, KCPD Psychologist Kay White, Sergeant Ward Smith, Captain Natalina Ehlers, Sergeant DeEtta Jacobs, and my coauthor, Chip). In addition, providential circumstances have sustained our efforts. I realize that the entire process could unravel at any time and frequently seems to be unraveling—but how can we throw up our hands and stop? Compelled by the very high core values we are discovering and advocating we haltingly press on.

Conceptual Structure

To conceptualize this environmental structure view of an organization, the pyramid illustration used in Chapter 2 (please refer to Figure 2.1) will be referred to once again. Keep in mind some basic presuppositions:

1. All problems at the upper levels of the pyramid ultimately exist or dissipate contingent on the lowest level. To explain, consider this extended definition of *integrity* as it applies to the base of the pyramid: to discern right from wrong regardless of my own biases, fears, prejudices, loyalties, schemas, and justifications. If all the decision makers and all the members always acted with complete integrity (which is humanly impossible), it would eventually create systems, redundancies, and attrition so as to functionally eliminate all human-related errors and social erosions.

* See http://abcnews.go.com/US/story?id=6376209&page=1.

2. The tip of the pyramid is distinct (it represents proactive response to problems that are discovered latent in the various environments when something goes wrong). The tip will at first get much attention but should eventually be the least focused on. As was just mentioned, when anything goes wrong, it creates a unique opportunity to detect flaws covertly embedded in the environmental systems of the organization. This is because law enforcement tends to be reactive (rather than proactive) and outcome focused (rather than process focused). That is to say, unless something goes wrong to the point of costing us something, "No harm—no foul." In other words, if I typically talk to citizens in a rude and condescending manner, as long as no complaints are substantiated, the behavior tends to be ignored. The problem with ignoring destructive attitudes and behaviors is this: whatever you don't address, you encourage. Unaddressed behavior becomes a psychological and social contract with much more influence than the organization's stated policies that are not uniformly enforced. If someone is rude and condescending and it is not addressed, it actually becomes a flaw in the social environment of the organization and creates a link to a potential catastrophe (see Chapter 4 for such a tragedy). Doing a root cause or system analysis evaluation does not imply that officers have no personal accountability for their behaviors. On the contrary, if one of the problems lies in the anima (integrity) of the individual, this individual must be invested in, in terms of mentoring, training, and support; then, if or when called for, dealt with decisively and be graciously allowed to find a profession that does not demand high character (as does law enforcement). This is a critical issue. Here is my experience: often, when commanders hear of a root cause or systems analysis process, they hear, "Oh, you are making excuses for the officers—you are helping them to avoid personal accountability." Nothing could be further from the truth. Identifying systemic problems and self-deceptions embedded into the organization is all about accountability. *Someone IS accountable for systemic failure at each level, and that is exactly what some commanders do not want exposed.* If your organization is unwilling to put the performance and decision making of *all* members up for scrutiny, you might as well put this book down now and cease to waste your time.

Once again, please refer back to Figure 2.1 in Chapter 2. Everything below the tip of the pyramid shown must be designed and relentlessly evaluated so that it causes things to go right. Please keep referring back to Figure 2.1 as we take a deeper look at the organizational environmental pyramid.

Brief Overview of Each Level

- The *functional environment* has to do with the equipment, tools, and machines that members interface with along with the physical (building, roads, vehicles, etc.) environment.
- The *structural environment* has to do with the written documents, policies, discipline processes, evaluation process, training processes, and so on.
- The *social environment* has to do with the traditions, norms, values, customs, heroes, schemas, groupthink, cliques, loyalties, and so on of the organization.
- The *anima environment* has to do with individuals. Stated in positive terms, it is personal integrity (ability and willingness to discern right from wrong and honor the personhood of every person) and courage (willingness to act for what is right toward all people, regardless of social and other pressures to the contrary). Stated in negative terms, it is self-deceptions (blinding internal justifications to act with malice, cowardice, or neglect toward others).

Anima Environment

In the form of a question, "How does an organization create an environment that builds and develops the anima of each individual member?" the short answer is as follows: the organization must hire, train, and have relentless accountability around the fact that *the profession of law enforcement requires a personal anima (inner way) that sees people as people, and is rooted in integrity, buttressed by courage, and expressed as unconditional respect for all.* Because this entire book has been demonstrating the importance of these aspects, and they build on each other, I will generally only refer to implementation processes in this chapter. Chapter 2 contains a series of diagrams under the Rule of 30 that illustrates this material (see Figure 2.2a–2.2j), and it should be reviewed by the reader at this time. I will mention several books and specific training processes that I know to be very good; I am sure there are other quality resources that accomplish the same purpose, but I am simply expressing this from my knowledge and experience base.

Pre-Employment

As applicants are working through the process of employment, they should be directed to obtain and read a copy of *Courage: The Backbone of Leadership* by Gus and Diane Lee. They should then write a brief overview of high core values, the courageous leadership model, and personal accountability around these issues. This paper should become part of their pre-employment jacket, and interview questions should focus on personal accountability around the content. No one should be hired who does not state a willingness to align themselves with high core values.

To support this effort, everyone involved in hiring and training (from the top commander to every officer and clerk) needs to take a course like the one we at the KCPD Leadership Academy call "High Core Values for Courageous Communications." Here are the basics of the course: as pre-work for the course, participants read, outline key chapters in, and do the "character quotient" in *Courage: The Backbone of Leadership*. During the five days of the course, participants are immersed in the concept of high core values (integrity, courage, and character). The goal is that when each member exits, he or she will:

- Understand high core values (HCV) and the inspirational nature they possess
- Have built systems of personal accountability around the implementation of HCV into his or her life and workplace
- Have skill sets for effectively communicating HCV both verbally and in writing

To accomplish these ends, during the course members are responsible for completing a group project to facilitate learning on a critical concept from the book, one of which includes the CLEAR (Communicate collegially, Listen actively with Empathy, Ask questions on point, and Relate respectfully) communications model for having courageous, relevant, respectful dialog. Members are also put through a professional writing course (we use FranklinCovey's Writing Advantage—each member receives not only sound instruction on how to write clearly, concisely, and effectively but also a professional style guide). All members then complete a "High Core Values Application Paper" that demonstrates (1) their commitment and process (including "buddy check," a process where you invite strategic partners to help you check your moral blind spots for lapses in integrity), which become lead measures on the path to building personal integrity, courage, and character; (2) how that becomes inspirational to the organization (lag measures); and (3) how to cascade and institutionalize HCV into their assignment. One such paper written in a class at the KCPD Leadership Academy was actually folded into the Duty Manual of the KCPD Personnel Section. During the class time, the paper in various stages of completion is read and evaluated by a different member of the class, with an in-depth discussion on the application of high core values following. To complete the class, the paper must be taken back to the workplace and be read and discussed by the member's immediate supervisor and at least one direct report (or coworker). And finally, once again hold discussions about establishing and maintaining HCV in the workplace.

To ensure a HCV hiring process, all members must then work together to establish an environment where a "buddy check" is normative and expected and *entrench high core values into every aspect of their work, particularly all selection and hiring processes.*

Once Employed

Once hired, *all members* should receive the Arbinger Institute's training courses "Choice" and "Choice @ Work." These courses have the option of coming with the books *Leadership and Self-Deception: Getting out of the Box* and *Anatomy of Peace.* These books *should be read* as part of the course prework (*Leadership and Self-Deception*) and post work (*Anatomy of Peace*). The third day of this training block should be a strategic communications course built around the anima we advocate, the "Peace Pyramid," and the CLEAR courageous communication model from *Courage: The Backbone of Leadership.* As members' careers develop, the "Choice" and "Choice @ Work" content should be regularly revisited to be kept fresh and applicable to their varying assignments. Also, for example, instructors and field training officers should receive the course "Choice in Education," and those involved in mentoring, coaching, mediation, or negotiation should receive "Choice in Intervention." Members should also receive yearly refreshers on the strategic communications model.

All members must be seen and developed as leaders and should receive "High Core Values for Courageous Communications," as described above, within the first few years of employment. As they progress into supervisory and management roles, they should receive training that further develops their effectiveness such as FranklinCovey's "The 7 Habits for Law Enforcement" and "Leadership: Great Leaders, Great Teams, Great Results." The way we utilize the FranklinCovey Leadership course in captains' school (for sergeants who have completed the testing phase and are going to be put on the list for promotion to captain—assuming they pass the school) is that I set the context for the school by setting up an imaginary scenario for the first five days of the school:

> It is your first day as a new patrol captain. You are excited to meet your new Major, and now he/she is going to arrive to address the class—listen as if you are the only one who is being addressed. When the Major arrives, he/she is extremely irate after being humiliated when a commendation recommendation went up the chain of command with the previous captain. The write-up has come back down with a request to resolve what appears to be a policy violation that precipitated the event. The major wants "heads to roll" so this does not

happen again. The new captain soon finds out that not only is the major angry, but also rumor has already hit the rank and file, and they are fearful and angry. Trust is at an all-time low, and work productivity is drastically down. As the issue is studied, it becomes apparent that the entire division had been working out of an operational understanding of the policy, which is not aligned with the stated policy, and no one really understands what the problem is. The class is divided into work groups, and each work group has a current captain as a group mentor. As the leadership material is covered, the captain is with the group to help individuals to understand how the principles fit into this real-life scenario and give them a basis of turning this problem into an opportunity to clarify purpose, align systems, inspire trust, and unleash talent. The candidates then use the time in class to create an action plan complete with lead and lag measures. However, before the candidate can implement the plan, the irate major must be convinced that this plan is much better than ignoring the underlying causes and disciplining the officers. To do this, the candidates are taught the CLEAR communications model from the book *Courage* and are given an opportunity to practice it with classmates. The last day of class consists of completing the action plan and having an observed performance (the mentor captain is the evaluator) role-play with one of several majors who come in to be actors. The participants are evaluated on their ability to create an action plan based on the Four Imperatives and have a courageous, relevant conversation with an irate major following the CLEAR model.

Every opportunity must be taken to develop members' character and set an organizational norm for acting for what is right, especially when social norms are against it. The development of personal anima must be relentlessly pursued with high-quality training, intentionally linked to the highest organizational priorities and high core values.

At the KCPD, we further support the anima environment with a sergeant school that has many similarities to the format of the captain's school. It is built on "Choice" and "Choice @ Work" along with judgment interference factor initiative (JIFI) training. It contains a CLEAR observed performance with an "irate, closed minded Captain" and a writing project (Writing Advantage) to mitigate a systemic judgment interference factor and brooding cynicism.

In the 2009 in-service training, every law enforcement member received a four-hour course titled "Foundations for Strategic Awareness" that captures the critical concepts of this book (unconditional respect along with the tactical and interpersonal benefits).

Social Environment

All the work done above to foster and support the personal anima of individual members will be for naught if the social, structural and functional environments do not support the process and the people (refer again to the Rule of

30 in Chapter 2; and see Figure 2.2a–2.2j). *Personal anima and accountability are areas where those in management, especially the executive team, who typically have less accountability and transparency in police cultures, must have more.* Members must know this *before* going into management. If this is not true, cynicism, apathy, and distrust will grow and spread like gangrene, rotting everything it touches.

Three "Check-Up" Questions

In a safe, anonymous manner, ask each member the following questions to give your organization a quick check-up:

- I feel my organization fosters safe, open, honest, communication that is respectful of differing opinions and results in better ideas.
- I feel that all members of my organization are held accountable for results from top to bottom.
- I feel that I can fully trust my organization.*

Ask members to assign a numeric value that represents their level of agreement with each statement from 0 (*totally disagree*) to 10 (*totally agree*). Have them add their numbers together and divide by three for their average. Gather the resulting numbers and create an overall average. It is my personal opinion that if the overall average is not at least a 7, the organization is silently bleeding; below 5, the organization is hemorrhaging; and below 3, the organizations has flatlined and the following is likely true:

- People feel like they are seen and treated as objects—in such situations, they will do likewise to each other and community members (refer to Chapter 2).
- Trust is low.
- Cynicism is high.
- Opportunities are lost.
- Talent and creative energy are lying dormant beneath a sea of suspicion.
- Gossip and rumors are running and ruining everything.

Stopping the Bleeding

First, if the management team has not had the benefit of the series of courses comprising "Choice," "Choice @ Work," and "High Core Values for Courageous Communications," that is a good place to begin. Even if they

---

* For a more comprehensive look at this concept, see FranklinCovey's "Four Disciplines of Execution."

have, it should be revisited in the manner prescribed below. All commanders should understand that they have responsibility not only for their own character but also for the overall social and structural well-being of the organization, particularly their direct span of influence and responsibility. If the social environment is bleeding with cynicism, commanders (and all members, for that matter) desperately need to escape their own self-deception (see Chapter 2) and be honest within their selves, maybe for the first time. To do so, I would recommend that the executive staff take the "Choice" and "Choice @ Work" courses as a three-day course with influential, respected, and trusted members of the rank and file (identified by the rank and file) and members who represent any labor group. The goal is to create an "out-of-the-box" place where real communication and real understanding can take place. The last half of the second day should focus on "solving workplace collusions." The organization should identify trusted, realistic, *brutally honest* community members—and a few of them should be invited to the course (no more than 30 people total). The third day should be a judgment interference factor initiative (JIFI) overview (this chapter will later explain the JIFI). After this group gains some problem-solving momentum, to keep it going I would recommend that from this larger group, a smaller "Strike Force" be put together (about 15–20 people). This group should consist of roughly equal numbers from the executive staff and labor, and two or three from the community. This group would take the entire course "High Core Values for Courageous Communication" with all individual "High Core Value Application Papers" being directed at (1) building and instilling the writers' personal integrity, courage, and accountability; (2) cascading high core values into the organization as an inspirational social contagion; and (3) detailed plans for solving one area of the organization's most pressing problems (identified in the previous course as workplace collusions). Again, as part of the course, the papers are being shared, proofread, and discussed at every stage of completion. These papers should be presented and acted upon at all levels of the organization as soon as possible—to stop the bleeding.

The goal of the problem-solving groups would be to foster an organizational culture that:

- Is rooted in high core values
- Sees and treats all people as people
- Supports acting for what is right (courageous leadership)
- Fosters safe, open, honest communication (CLEAR)
- Has transparent accountability from *top to bottom* so that those who "refuse at the door" can be removed (see the Rule of 30 in Chapter 2)
- Considers the "buddy check" to be normative
- Eliminates the blue wall of silence, or *omerta* (an organized crime code of silence)

Gossip and Rumor Mitigation

All the above processes should work to create a social environment that is rooted in high core values and acts upon them relentlessly. All members would be trained and expected to engage in courageous, respectful, relevant conversations rooted in enduring principles of right and wrong. Gossip and rumors must be exposed for the caustic poison that they are, and be proactively rooted out.

Another way of accomplishing this is to instill a program where key members (people recognized by their peers as trustworthy and influential) in each division have an "open line" up the command chain to one designated commander (each commander would have two or three people who had the open line to contact them with gossip and rumors) with the expectations that gossip and rumors will be reported, addressed, and mitigated.

High Core Values and Basic Mission Alignment

The following images use the concept of sight alignment to illustrate a very important concept for establishing and maintaining alignment between organizational values and mission. Consider two other professions where mistakes cost lives, aviation and medicine: rigid hierarchical structures have been found to compromise aircraft safety. As a result, aviation professionals have intentionally taught shy junior cockpit crew members to speak up and veterans to receive this input.* Medicine has discovered that a solid process to keep from infecting patients with dangerous, sometimes deadly, secondary infections is a simple checklist. To be effectively utilized, all members are encouraged to participate regardless of rank structures.† *Some basics are so important that traditional hierarchical structures actually compromise lives.* What this advocates is the idea that high core values and basic mission are so important that the organization must be "flat" around these things. It's like washing your hands before surgery. It does not matter if you're the most renowned chief surgeon on staff or a newly hired nurse; you have to wash your hands. It is an absurdity to think otherwise—but thinking otherwise is exactly what hierarchical structures in policing lead to in so many cases. Everyone (top to bottom) hides behind authority structures as if authority

---

* Steven Robertson, "Rank in the Cockpit (communication between crew members during military aeronautical operations) (Brief Article)," Flying Safety, 2002, accessmylibrary, http://www.accessmylibrary.com/coms2/summary_0286-43018_ITM (accessed August 15, 2009).

† Atul Gawande, "The Checklist," New Yorker, 2007, http://www.newyorker.com/reporting/ 2007/12/10/071210fa_fact_gawande?currentPage=all (accessed August 15, 2009).

Rear Sight
High Core Values (HCV)

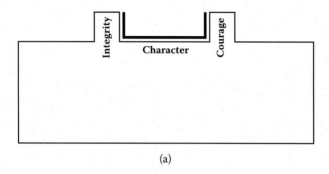

(a)

Front Sight
Basic Mission

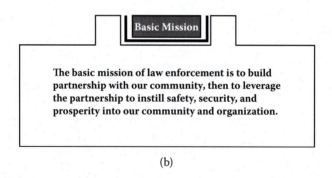

The basic mission of law enforcement is to build partnership with our community, then to leverage the partnership to instill safety, security, and prosperity into our community and organization.

(b)

A mission, objective, position, or action is legitimate only if it can be aligned with *both* HCV and the basic mission.

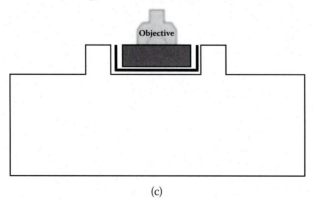

(c)

Figure 9.1

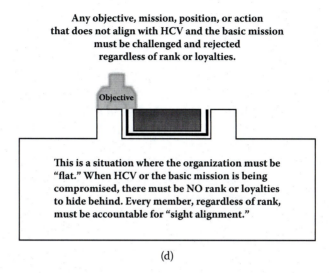

Any objective, mission, position, or action that does not align with HCV and the basic mission must be challenged and rejected regardless of rank or loyalties.

Objective

This is a situation where the organization must be "flat." When HCV or the basic mission is being compromised, there must be NO rank or loyalties to hide behind. Every member, regardless of rank, must be accountable for "sight alignment."

(d)

Figure 9.1 (Continued)

makes wrong right. Take a few moments to look over and read the "sight alignment" diagrams (Figure 9.1a–9.1d).

Judgment Interference Factor Initiative (JIFI)

The judgment interference factor initiative (JIFI) can be defined as follows:

> The identification and mitigation of factors that link the tasks of law enforcement to complaints, litigation, loss of community trust and support, internal cynicism, damage and destruction of equipment and resources, injuries, deaths, riots, and catastrophes.

Another issue that must be addressed regarding the social environment of an organization is for it to have awareness, and proactive elimination, of judgment interference factors (see Chapter 4's reference to unintended consequences in training processes as an example). On the KCPD, the JIFI is the vehicle that is seeking to address this important issue. As this initiative is groundbreaking in the field of law enforcement and is still in the formative stages, I will use historical narrative to explain it.

The first significant event in this historical account was one of the research projects that fell to me (I was off on the day it came up). The project involved the training for, and deployment of, personal protective equipment (PPE) that the KCPD had been given through the Department of Homeland Security post September 11, 2001. I was confronted with many issues (which were largely being ignored) related to spirometer (an instrument that measures the volume of air entering and leaving the lungs to verify minimum capacity) certification, fitting, donning (without cutting off circulation to extremities), training (considering extreme sensations of claustrophobia—tactical dexterity problems, hydration, heat stroke, and communicating), and decontaminating (which you cannot do with our issued leather gear). During this time, I visited with a friend, Robert Carroll, who was a maintenance engineer trainer in the airlines industry. He told me that I was dealing with issues known as *human factors* or *judgment interference factors*. Robert was amazed that given my position as a trainer on a large police department, I had never heard of the concept. Robert and his supervisor, Steve Ghidoni, graciously arranged to present their one-day course, "Human Factors in Airline Maintenance," to a group of law enforcement personnel. I pulled together a group of personnel with a diverse background in law enforcement and with well over a century of combined experience. During the course, the trainers introduced twelve factors that they affectionately call the *Dirty Dozen*:

- Lack of communication
- Norms
- Fatigue
- Stress
- Lack of recourses
- Lack of teamwork
- Lack of knowledge
- Lack of awareness
- Distraction (becoming channeled)
- Complacency
- Pressure: internal and external
- Lack of assertiveness

These twelve factors act as causal links between daily tasks and catastrophes. The argument is that when a task becomes catastrophic due to human error (which is frequently the source), there are always at least four of the twelve factors present and usually around eight. The factors act as causal links, so the power is in the idea that you only have to identify and mitigate *one of the factors and the catastrophe is averted*. This principle alone represents both a great opportunity and a *critical roadblock to a reactionary, outcome-focused culture such as law enforcement*, because you can't prove a negative. For example, during the class I was amazed to learn that the worst aviation accident in history, in which over 578 people were killed, had as some of its primary causal human factors poor communication and lack of assertiveness. This accident occurred on March 27, 1977, when KLM 747-200 and Pan Am 747-100 collided on the runway of the airport at Tenerife, Canary Islands. *If* the copilot would have acted with moral courage, and not let the pilot take off, the accident would not have happened. *But* the copilot would probably have lost his job. Why? *Because you can't prove he saved 578 people if no collision happens.* The only things that could have been proved would have been that he embarrassed and enraged the most revered "on-time" pilot in that particular airline, and he caused a large airliner full of people to become stranded with a costly flight delay. Here is where I make a huge distinction from the airline industry in the error chain concept. I firmly believe that the individual factors (perils) stand in the error chain like pearls on a string. If the string is broken, the entire error chain collapses. The "string" upon which all these "perils" ride is self-deception (see Figure 9.2). That is why I keep referring back to the Rule of 30 in Chapter 2 (Figure 2.2a–2.2j). An organization must always support acting for what is right on four levels: (1) *personal anima* development; (2) *social support*; (3) *structural support*—policies, training, and systems; and (4) *functional support*. See also the sight alignment diagrams (Figure 9.1a–9.1d).

After the human factors training, I surveyed the group of personnel who had attended (the group represented well over a century of combined experience in practically every area of law enforcement) with one question: "Do you feel that judgment interference factors, or something like them, bear upon police work, and link the tasks of police work to problems and catastrophes?" The answer was unanimously yes.

I then conducted an effort to find out if anyone on the KCPD knew of human factors, considered them, and proactively attempted to mitigate them to diminish problems and catastrophes, thus protecting KCPD personnel and the members of our community. The answer was no.

Obviously if there is no awareness, there can be no mitigation tactics. This presents an unacceptable hazard, places the members of the KCPD and the community in unnecessary peril, and leaves the agency exposed to untold civil litigation costs. I then began an informal survey of all the national police leaders

String of Perils

The "string" that supports each of these perils and allows tasks to link to catastrophe is **self deception:**

Blinding presuppositions and schemas, that are fortified with personal justifications and / or blame directed at others. Left unchallenged self deception becomes mindless (not safe to discuss or disagree) groupthink.

Task | Lack of resources · Norms · Complacency · Pressure · Distraction · Fatigue | Catastrophe

Remove the string and the *entire error chain evaporates*.
None of the links stand, no error chain exists.

Mitigation tactics should be directed at identifying and mitigating each individual peril BUT primary effort should always be directed at eliminating the "string" that all the perils ride upon.

The only way to effectively interact with the "String of Perils" is to first assume "*My* self deception is the string."

Figure 9.2

and trainers I had contact with as part of my duties. Every indication was that there is no widespread formal awareness, tracking, or intentional mitigation of judgment interference factors in law enforcement. A few progressive organizations have a "risk management" office, but most of those activities are directed at what has gone wrong, not proactively helping things go right by identifying and mitigating causal links at all critical organizational levels.

This realization began a long-term campaign for me: attempting to get the KCPD or someone in law enforcement to formally research and implement a JIFI. Some years later, the initiative finally found political traction as a subset of the "Blue Print for the Future—Management and Decision Making Committee," and has become part of the *animat*ing process of the larger initiative captured in this book. I need to mention here the direct correlation to the issue of unconditional respect. The number one cause of organizational errors is related to ineffective communication. The quickest and most reliable way to overcome the obstacles related to communication breakdown is unconditional respect rooted in integrity and buttressed by courage. Once again, by the time this book is published, the KCPD initiative that I began should have at least some overview training available to other organizations through the efforts of Bryan Courtney, director of the Missouri Regional Center for Public Safety and the Bureau of Justice Assistance (who are assisting our efforts). Their website can be visited at http://www.missouriwestern.edu/rcpi/.

The basis of factor identification and mitigation is going to be founded in the concepts put forward in this chapter. It will eventually involve the following:

1. Establishing the understanding that all the judgment interference factors (the Dirty Dozen-or some law enforcement specific hybrid) ultimately ride on self-justifications that become self-deception. For example:
   - I know that the slicer comes with a blade guard, but it does not really work for me—I will be safe.
   - I know that I have been awake for twenty-six hours straight, but I will be able to safely drive my family home through the night.
   - It's OK for me to go a hundred miles per hour just for the fun of it; I am the police, so therefore I know what I am doing.
   - I know that Officer Smith is treating citizens like crap, but that is not my problem; he has a sergeant—so it is his sergeant's responsibility, not mine.
   - It is OK to lie on a report to put a "bad guy" in jail; it serves the greater good.
2. Developing a matrix that provides solid processes for identifying and mitigating factors at the individual and workgroup levels.
3. Gathering solid data that demonstrate the problematic nature of the factor (such as current research on fatigue). Then, if the factor is

organizationally systemic (nothing can be done at the individual or work group level to mitigate it), a high-quality document can easily be put together (cut and paste from the matrix).

Not all factors can be eliminated (they are part of the job), but the detrimental effect can be assuaged when factors are identified (brought out into the light of day) and dealt with intentionally.

The JIFI process will also include awareness and *daily* training around high-risk, low-frequency, no-discretion-time (HR/LF/NDT) events that require officers to apply volumes of policies and skill sets during tense, uncertain, and rapidly evolving circumstances. For example, if an officer sees another officer using what appears to be unreasonable force, but can't possibly know everything the other officer knows (e.g., an uncontrolled hand hidden under the body has a gun), what is the response? Under a JIFI process, work groups would identify their HR/LF/NDT events, and work with experts in the area to create standardized, realistic, ongoing training (SVROT) that is verified in both content and frequency. Gordon Graham* makes a great case that this type of training should be daily and last only a few minutes. Every day is training day—dealing with one of the identified HR/LF/NDT events in a manner that relentlessly reinforces high core values and basic mission. Training times are systematically rotated so that each month, every event is trained on several times.

- As way of reminder, all problems should trigger a red team look at every aspect of organizational structure and processes. *Red teaming* is a structured and iterative process executed by trained, educated, and practiced team members with access to relevant subject matter expertise, uniquely suited for critical analysis. Red teaming provides decision makers with an independent capability to continuously challenge
  - Operational environment assumptions
  - Plans and operations from partner and adversary perspectives[†]

---

[*] A former California Highway Patrol officer, attorney, and risk management expert, Gordon Graham has popularized the practice of high-risk, low frequency, no-discretion-time awareness and training.

[†] Adapted from Gregory Fontenot (U.S. Army colonel, ret.), "Seeing Red: Creating a Red-Team Capability for the Blue Force," Military Review (September–October 2005): http://usacac.army.mil/CAC/milreview/English/SepOct05/SEPOCT05/fontenot.pdf (accessed June 6, 2009). I (Jack Colwell) appreciate Mr. Gregory Fontenot, who allotted me the privilege of attending the six-week "Red Team Members Course" at the University of Foreign Military and Cultural Studies at Fort Leavenworth, Kansas. This type of training should become normative in law enforcement—a culture endemic with "we have always done it this way" blinding presuppositions and groupthink.

Everything and everyone (except the high core values and basic mission) should be on the table for scrutiny—no "Wizard of Oz" behind the curtain who can't be looked at, and no "sacred cow" process that can't be eliminated.

Community Feedback

The three check-up questions presented earlier could give an organization a simple way to give itself an internal social environment evaluation (FranklinCovey's "4 Disciplines of Execution" would give a comprehensive check-up), but a decisive question still remains: Is every contact with every member of our community being effectively utilized to build partnership around the basic mission of law enforcement?* I am not really talking about the worn-out phrase *customer service*. I am referring to the simple concept of *do community members feel like they have been seen as people and treated with unconditional respect?* (See Chapter 6.) Obviously, this creates a cultural and structural shift in the way law enforcement has typically done business. From Chapter 7, it takes the job of "bean counting"—the statistical analysis of work productivity—out of the realm of the simple, lazy process of counting enforcement activities in prescribed areas. This is because the focus is no longer on lead measures like staffing, car checks, pedestrian checks, search warrants, and so on. I recommend that new lead measures come from having an independent arm apart from the organization constantly giving a random selection of community members a simple follow-up that looks something like this (this will obviously have to be changed or honed with actual experience in your area):

> Good afternoon, I am Joe Smith with our city's Community Partnership Team. Our records indicate that Officer Jones has left your residence, where you reported a burglary. Could I ask you two brief questions, please? Based on the service you have received, on a scale of one to ten, how likely would it be that you would recommend that a friend or relative move to our community? (Response in the form of a number.) Can you briefly explain why you rated us this way, please?

Something like this should be done to get a random cross section from those who receive service from every division on every watch, go to every facility for any reason, and deal with members at *every rank*. Something like this should even be directed at those who receive traffic tickets and are arrested. Responses should primarily be used as lag measures that will provide critical feedback on the current anima and social environments (see the pyramid in Figure 1.1) of the organization and the resulting effectiveness of partnership

---

* A great resource for consideration of this concept is Fred Reichheld, The Ultimate Question: Driving Good Profits and True Growth (Boston: Harvard Business School Press, 2006).

building with the community. The primary purpose of the feedback is to allow the *organization* to self-correct—*not* to identity problem members. Obviously some responses may warrant additional support and training and occasionally an internal investigation, but even the result of those should precipitate a process of "proactively addressing what has gone wrong" by pushing down the pyramid, and looking for and fixing dysfunction at every level.

The above lead measure (direct community survey immediately following police contact) will feed the collection of data (community member responses) that should be predictive of the effectiveness (or ineffectiveness) of the basic mission—build community partnership. Combined, these should be predictive of the final goal—safety, security, and prosperity within our community (see Chapter 7).

I believe that another great lag measure that should be part an organizational evaluation process would be the recruitment and retention of many high-quality minority individuals from our communities. People would naturally want to work for an organization where current members see you as a person and treat you with respect, which unleashes your creative energy around a common purpose.

Structural Environment

This refers to the organization's written documents: its mission, purpose, strategic plan, values, policies, special orders, and so on.

Whenever any problem is manifest at the tip of the pyramid, all related training, policies, and documents should be "red-teamed." Below are the criteria that drive the evaluation.

Documents Must Be Rooted in High Core Values and Support the Basic Mission

All policies must support acting for what is right (again, see the Rule of 30 in Chapter 2, Figure 2.1a–2.1j) and create a "sight alignment" between basic mission and high core values (Figure 9.1a–9.1d). To accomplish this, all members who write or review policies need to go through the same "High Core Values for Courageous Communications" course described earlier for those working in personnel. Each High Core Values Application Paper should, once again, demonstrate the following: (1) the individual's commitment and process (including a "buddy check" system) to build his or her personal integrity, courage, and character (lead measures); (2) how that becomes inspirational to the organization (lag measures); and (3) how to cascade and institutionalize high core values into the assignment (writing of policies).

Documents Must Be Unambiguous

Once the documents are written and vetted for high core values at every level, they should be reviewed by the "end users" to verify they are understood in the same way they are meant to be understood. I can tell you of two experiences where people who were involved in writing a policy that had been utilized for years were later in a debate about what the policy actually said. In each of the two situations, the dumbfounded writer found himself saying, "That's not what it's supposed to say." If an officer, along with the entire division, is working on a good-faith understanding of an ambiguously written policy, no one really knows or cares until there is a bad outcome (see the situation involving the firing of the two officers in Chapter 4). If you "hammer" the officers with the intended meaning of an ambiguous policy, you will spread fear, cynicism, and apathy. Therefore, documents must be carefully written and vetted for clarity and ease of interpretation by those who must abide by them.

Documents Must Be Seamlessly Linked to Operational Norms

Once the documents are rooted in high core values and vetted to demonstrate that they are clearly written in unambiguous language, there must be a seamless link between the document and operational norms (what is actually happening in the field). Absent this seamless link, operational norms become psychological and social contracts within the organization that eclipse socially unsupported written documents. Once again, typically if an officer, along with the entire division, is working under operational norms that are not aligned with the written policy, no one really knows or cares until there is a bad outcome. Again, if you "hammer" the officers with the stated policy, you will create a cascade of personnel problems. Some even argue that this type of action leads to dramatic increases in crime because officers disengage out of fear.*

Documents Must Be under Constant Scrutiny and Constantly Improved

If an operational normative has usurped the written policy, they should both be reexamined to determine which is more solidly rooted in high core values and in keeping with the organization's highest priorities. Then realignment must occur.

---

* Dr. Ernest Evans, quoted in Jack Cashill, "The Etiquette of Economic Distress," Ingrams Online Magazine, April 2009, http://www.ingramsonline.com/March_2008/index.php.

All Evaluation Processes Must Be Linked to the Organization's *Stated* Values and Priorities

This book has said much about this, so I won't belabor the issue. It suffices to say that while almost all agencies' organizational values and mission statements align with Peelian principles, almost none of the evaluation processes are linked to the mission statement or values. Most of the "bean counting" takes the lazy, easy way out of counting activity, not results. Misalignment of evaluation processes is another situation where improper configuration can exist and will set the stage for continuous confusion, fear, and apathy. Evaluation processes should be under the constant scrutiny of the red team.

All Training Processes Must Be Constantly Scrutinized for Unintentional Consequences

See Chapter 4 for an example of unintended consequences of training. For this reason, all related training processes should be red-teamed whenever problems manifest themselves at the tip of the pyramid.

Functional Environment

Again, refer the Rule of 30 (see Figure 2.2a–2.2j) for an example of the importance of the functional environment. One should also consider the impact that the physical appearance of homes and yards in neighborhoods has on criminal activity as a functional environment issue. For now, let us focus on the officer doing the job.

Today, officers are interfacing with an ever more complicated array of devices and equipment. It seems as though the totality of expectations that are placed on officers by this vast array of interfaces is rooted in a fictional view of whom and what humans are.

To Err Is Human

People make errors almost as routinely as they breathe. Most of these errors do not become an issue, but some do; in fact, a "General Accounting Office (GAO) report ... cited human error rates as a key (in the range of 50 percent) factor in major system failures."[*] There are two basic types of errors: slips and mistakes.

---

[*] James A. Pharmer, "The Challenges and Opportunities of Implementing Human Systems Integration into the Navy Acquisitions Process," Defense A R Journal, February 1, 2007, http://www.accessmylibrary.com/coms2/summary_0286-32681766_ITM (accessed September 4, 2009). Note also that the GAO is now the Government Accountability Office.

Slips are automatic subconscious behaviors (like something as innocuous as pressing the wrong key when keyboarding, or as devastating as drawing a handgun when a conducted energy weapon was intended). Slips are made without thought or deliberation.

Mistakes are with conscious deliberation. Many of the very traits that make humans creative, insightful, flexible, and responsive will also cause us to leap to faulty or incorrect conclusions.*

Both of these error types are significantly influenced by human interaction with everything in their environment. Becoming proactive in this area requires that before equipment is purchased, it be vetted to ensure the design meets the realities of human performance capability. "These capabilities include cognitive, physical, and sensory skills required for training and using a system."† Remaining proactive requires that when there is a problem, the human–equipment interface is examined for possible causal links. This is science; it is not a scapegoat hunt. It is exactly the opposite; without such an investigation, the *human is* the scapegoat—and this is the foundation for endless error cycles, and for fear and cynicism by the equipment users who are injured and/or disciplined regarding the errors.

For an extreme example, review the issues I raised on spirometer certification, fitting, donning, training, and decontaminating. Imagine the "train wreck" of having a catastrophe that requires putting large amounts of officers in PPE. The officers are unfamiliar with the PPE environment and have no idea about their respiratory, heat, tactile, tactical, and equipment limitations. It is a 90°F day with bright sunshine. The officers put the suit on over their uniforms minus their leather gear. The suit is taped; many of the officers begin to feel claustrophobic, and some become slightly oxygen deprived because of stress response breathing. Their clothing and body begin to swell as the internal suit temperature instantly begins to soar, causing profuse sweating; the swelling cuts off circulation where the tape was applied. They quickly realize that the leather equipment does not secure to the outside of the suit well, and they have very limited dexterity to use the equipment. As some begin to have the first signs of heat stroke, the portable communication devices are found to be worthless, and the untested water intake system does not work. The officers are then rapidly deployed into a dangerous situation that *just became exponentially worse.* The easy scapegoat would be to blame the deployed officers

---

* Donald A. Norman, The Design of Everyday Things (New York: Basic Books, 2002), 105.
† J. J. Clark and R. K. Goulder, "Human Systems Integration (HSI): Ensuring Design and Development Meet Human Performance Capability Early in Acquisition Process (the Acquisition Process)," Program Manager 31, no. 4 (July–August 2002): 88; and InfoTrac Military & Intelligence via Gale, http://find.galegroup.com/itx/start.do?prodId=SPJ.SP02 (retrieved March 6, 2009).

for bad decisions, tactical failures, and the ensuing nightmare of chain reaction events.

For other examples of a functional environment in a police cruiser:

- All equipment placed in the cockpit must be vetted for the attention limitation realities of humans, not designed for an imaginarily perfect robot.
- Equipment like mobile data terminals and shotgun racks must be positioned to allow for ease of use and visibility, while not creating blind spots or additional danger for the officer during a collision.
- Simple additions to make entering an intersection while operating as an emergency vehicle (light and siren) safer. Such as installing a devise which gives the officer the ability to depress the horn to alternate the siren sound. The alternative is to either not have a siren variation (which decreases the likelihood of being noticed by other drivers) or the officer having to take attention away from the road and hands off the steering wheel to activate the function during a critical moment.

Summary

I suppose it has happened in law enforcement history, but I cannot think of a single incident where an organization has suffered the loss of an officer through death, injury, indictment, litigation, or employment action or prosecuted the wrong person and been:

- rightfully humiliated in the press
- successfully sued (or settled to avoid being sued)
- targeted by civil unrest
- endured great community distrust

where proactive responses in one of the listed four organizational environments could not have averted the catastrophe. Would someone care to calculate the costs associated with this? The consideration of this boggles my imagination.

With this in mind, one last reminder: all problems should trigger a red team look at every aspect of organizational structure and processes.

One of our KCPD deputy chiefs reported upon returning from the most recent International Association of Chiefs of Police conference that there was a brooding undercurrent in even our nation's premier police organizations. That undercurrent was low morale. I do not see this pervasive low morale as surprising, but as inevitable. At the same time, low morale is unnecessary. This chapter has laid out a comprehensive plan for *animating* a culture. I chose to capitalize on the term *anima* because the whole process is rooted in personal anima, especially that of the one who would begin to implement these changes. As the medical profession has found out repeatedly by painful trial and error, the one who would do deep, delicate surgery must have *clean hands and an open mind.* Otherwise, the "helper" will inadvertently become a purveyor of dysfunction and loss. So a personal anima inventory is critical here:

- Do I see those who I wish would change as people or as objects? Are their dreams and aspirations as important as mine are? Or are they simply obstacles to my success and need to change or move aside?
- Have I established my own integrity, and do I have a functional "buddy check" system in place?
- Have I developed and established my own character over time with consistent acts of integrity and courage?
- Have I consistently, over time, expressed my inner way as unconditional respect for all people?

If the answer to all these questions is "Yes—not perfectly, but growing each day," then you have the clean hands and the open mind to begin the deep, delicate surgery required to begin to *anima*te a culture. We wish you all the success and look forward to hearing great stories of transformed lives, organizations, and communities—stories with new heroes: heroes with deep integrity, moral courage, and unconditional respect for all.

Index

A

Abu Ghraib prison scandal, 4, 119
Abundance Mentality, 74
abuse of power, 46
Academic Advisory Council, 85
accountability
  building personal anima, 5, 129
  conflict-avoidant culture, 12
  passive defiance, 73
Achan (Biblical figure), 7
actions, perceived social grouping impact, 11
Adam-12 television series, 100–101
Adelson, Rachel, 53
aggression loop, 54
AIOE contra flu (Anima, rooted in Integrity that sees Others as people who are Equally important to us), 120–122
airlines incident, 134–135
alarm clock scenario, 68
American Psychological Association, 4, 119
Anatomy of Peace, 127
Andrews, Robert, 79
anima
  accountability, 129
  building, 5
  characteristics of developed, 114
  defined, 1, 25
  disregard of social context, 5
  etymology, 2
  listening, 57–58
  natural observance, 40
  purpose of use, 2
  questions, 144
  tactical benefits, 43–46
annual evaluations, 74
APA Online, 4, 119
appearance *vs.* being, 28
Arbinger principles
  anima, 57
  Better-Than Box, 15
  driver's license scenario, 50
  objectifying others, 16
  Pygmalion effect, 92
  training courses, 127
Arendt, Hannah, 8–9, 16
arrogance, lack of, 67
assumptions, 122
attention, 37
attentional blindness, 39
attention limits, *see* CHAFSBAD
attitude, lessons learned, 55, 57
"Automacticity of Emotion Recognition, The," 86
avarice, *see* CHAFSBAD
awareness importance, 135–136

B

Bandura, Albert, 58
Bassett, Danielle S., 87
Batson, C.D, 9
bean counting
  community feedback, 138
  misalignment of evaluation processes, 141
  winning hearts and minds, 98
Beaumont, Leland R., 54
behavior, justification, 110
benefits, tactical
  during contact, 37–40
  hesitation gap, closing, 41–43
  internal code (anima), 43–46
  precontact threat assessment, 34–37
  precursors of violence, awareness, 37–40
  respect, confusion of, 31–32
  respect, defining, 25–30
  unconditional respect, 32–34
  using force, 41–43
bias, 33, *see also* CHAFSBAD
Biggs, Mary, 79

Jack Colwell and Chip Huth have written a refreshing analysis of law enforcement in the twenty-first century. The authors make a sound case for the "personal anima" approach that sees all people as people and is rooted in integrity, reinforced by courage, and expressed through unconditional respect for all. Never has there been a time in policing that an approach such as "personal anima" is needed more. Colwell and Huth have struck a chord of innovation and crispness, which will assuredly provide a working framework for police authorities as they engage the challenges of policing dynamic communities of the twenty-first century. The book is impressively well referenced, and their writing style is clear and concise. More importantly, the book is written by two veteran police officers who know what they are talking about. Colwell and Huth's book is a must read for police practitioners and police scholars who wish to advance a new era of thinking about policing.

Michael Birzer
Director and Associate Professor
School of Community Affairs
Wichita State University

Unleashing the Power of Unconditional Respect is a must read book for all law enforcement trainers, FTO's and supervisors. The concepts of integrity, courage, and unconditional respect for all are critical elements in the development of law enforcement professionals, yet they reflect a gap in many of today's law enforcement training programs. This book is a positive step towards filling that gap.

Brian Willis
President, Winning Mind Training

Brian Willis retired from the Calgary Police Service in 2004 after 25 years service. He is the editor and contributing writer for the acclaimed books *W.I.N.: Critical Issues in Training and Leading Warriors, W.I.N. 2: Insights Into Training and Leading Warriors,* and a contributing writer for *Warriors: On Living with Courage, Discipline and Honor.* He is the Editor of the *ILEETA Review,* writes the *W.I.N. Column* for the *ILEETA Use of Force Journal and* has had numerous articles published in law enforcement periodicals. Brian has been featured on the Calibre Press Street Survival Newsline and on www.policeone.com for some of his innovative training programs. Brian also operates Warrior Spirit Books (www.warriorspiritbooks.com).

"Personal integrity ... unconditional respect for others ... moral courage: are they no longer valued in today's America? Veteran law enforcement officers Chip Huth and Jack Colwell discuss barriers and present practical guidelines in this call for a return to these key values. This book inspired me; all Americans should read it."

Debra Sheffer, Ph.D.
Associate Professor, History
Chair, University Assessment Committee
Park University

Officers Jack Colwell and Chip Huth have developed and proposed an eloquent argument on how best to improve policing at both the tactical and operational levels. They make the compelling—and, to outsiders, obvious—argument that IF police officers treat both citizens and perpetrators with unconditional respect, they will "serve and protect" better by orders of magnitude. Colwell and Huth seek nothing less than to effect a transformation of how we educate and train police officers. Their argument is well grounded, well supported, and compelling. This will be a classic in leadership education for first responders and any who seek to serve and protect. *Unleashing the Power of Unconditional Respect* conveys powerful ideas for all of us.

Colonel Gregory Fontenot, U.S. Army (retired),

Former director of the School of Advanced Military Studies, director of the University of Foreign Military Studies, and coauthor of *On Point: The US Army in Operation Iraqi Freedom*

Having been in law enforcement for thirty-five years, I know that our profession tends to define events not necessarily how they are, but how we think they ought to be. When we do this, it makes no difference if the interaction occurs on the street, in the squad room, or in our living room, for the result is often the same: our reaction is wrong. Colwell and Huth present us with an amalgam of theory, best practices, and sound advice that if followed will lead us down the path of transformation. We would do well to follow the map that they have provided for us.

Chief Gregory P. Mills
Director of Public Safety, Riverside Missouri

Director Mills retired as a commander from the KCPD with 29 years experience to include administration, patrol, investigations and media relations. He is a Graduate of the FBI National Academy, the Program For Senior Level Executives In State and Local Government, John F. Kennedy School of Government, Harvard University and holds a Master of Arts, Public Administration. Besides serving as the Director of Public Safety he is also

Adjunct Faculty, Park University: Online course developer; Criminal Justice in the Undergraduate School; Public Affairs in the Graduate School.

Colwell and Huth have written a book that deals with the very foundation not just of communication but of civil society. Their careful thought, lifetimes of service and insightful contribution will undoubtedly change the world for the better.

Joseph Grenny
NYT Bestselling co-author of Influencer: The Power to Change Anything

"Your shield is not a symbol of your authority over the community. It is a symbol of your subservience to that community." This thought underpins the thesis of a new book by warrior poets Jack Colwell and Chip Huth of the Kansas City Police Department. How we view ourselves and how it may differ from how the community views us comprise a pivotal point in this discussion ... unconditional respect must itself be conditioned, and this text tells you just how to do that. The principle objective of the police profession is to seek the public's willing compliance to social norms and to remove from that society those who will not conform. We interact with all walks and stations in life. We view them with the filters that our life's experience has given us. How we understand those filters is as important as the tactics and equipment we use. Those unconscious thoughts and manners are as valuable to a tactically well-rounded officer as body armor. They may well be considered a kind of body armor for the psyche.

I have undergone a training regimen this year that includes the precepts taught in this text, and I approve of it without reservation. This attitudinal recognition will make you a better police officer and a safer one.

Every enlightened law officer should read this book and then live it.

Col. Hugh L. Mills Jr.
Sheriff's Office, Jackson County, Missouri.
(US Army Ret.) Co-Author: Low Level Hell: A Scout Pilot in the Big Red One

Highest praise for *Unleashing the Power of Unconditional Respect* and the comprehensive analysis it provides. The authors offer a thorough assessment of the law enforcement community and the underlying problems that impede career excellence. Their provocative exploration into the human psyche encourages officers to more completely understand themselves, all the while providing empirical data that link this self-awareness to officer safety. They do not claim to have all the answers, but only ask the challenging questions that encourage officers to review their behavior and continually challenge their underlying motives. They invite all to lead by example and encourage every action to be "rooted in integrity, buttressed by courage, and expressed in unconditional respect for all persons." All of this to reach the ultimate goal of superior community relations, bringing the law enforcement organization back to its roots of "Protect and serve."

Kay White
MS, Forensic Psychology Associates
Psychologist for the Kansas City Missouri Police Department

In "Unleashing the Power of Unconditional Respect," Jack Colwell and Chip Huth have written a courageous book that will–for those of us who courageously embrace its message–forever change the way we do police work for the better. For those of us who genuinely appreciate the privilege granted us when we pin on the badge, and who truly believe our role in society to be a vital and honorable one, it will deepen our resolve to do our best and give us the tools we need to improve. For those who have fallen into the trap of discouragement and cynicism, it will show us the way out of that darkness and renew our belief in the fact that we can make a difference if we care enough to change. And for those of us who are privileged to lead, it will show us how to inspire our officers to protect and serve more effectively, and with courage and honor. I highly recommend it.

Brian McKenna
author of "Officer Down! Lessons from the Streets."
Warrior Spirit Books.

Brian retired as a lieutenant after 30 years with the Hazelwood Police Department and is the owner of WINNING EDGE TRAINING in the St. Louis MO area. Brian writes extensively on officer safety topics, and authors Law Officer Magazine's Officer Down column, a regular feature that analyzes officer-involved shootings for key learning points.

Law enforcement has long needed to hear the message offered in this book. Sometimes, in the heat of battle, or in the drudgery of day-to-day policing, we forget the most basic of cultural mores. When an officer's day involves moving from one tragic or violent event to the next, with all of the disappointing human interaction that such things involve, it's easy for him or her to lose sight of such issues as basic human dignity, self-worth, and respect. Huth and Colwell offer valuable insights into the effect that such a mindset can have on both personal and professional undertakings. If law enforcement can move toward a model of unconditional respect, many of our problems will become much easier to manage: Officers and citizens will be safer, community trust will grow, and our world will be a safer, saner place in which to live. I heartily recommend this book!

Steve Ashley
Use of Force Trainer and Risk Management Expert

"From the moment of reading the title of this book, I was hooked. As a public safety executive, I am constantly looking for ways to communicate our accountability and to keep our actions centered in integrity. In a world where dignity and respect are sought-after commodities, it was refreshing to read such a thoughtful and scholarly discourse on how to give and receive those gifts. I am recommending this book to law enforcement professionals as necessary reading."

Susan Rockett
Chief of Public Safety
Mexico, Missouri
President of the National Association of Women Law Enforcement Executives

"Threefold strength of profound philosophical depth, practical hard-won experience, and professional integrity. May all those entrusted with the safety and welfare of the public be inspired and guided."

Ivan Welch
Lieutenant Colonel, U.S. Army (retired)